ECUADOR

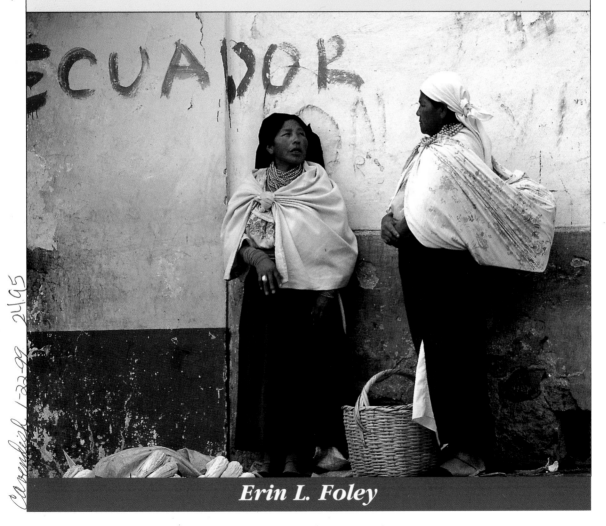

Erin L. Foley

MARSHALL CAVENDISH
New York • London • Sydney

Reference Edition published 1999 by
Marshall Cavendish Corporation
99 White Plains Road
Tarrytown
New York 10591

© Times Editions Pte Ltd 1995

Originated and designed by
Times Books International, an imprint of
Times Editions Pte Ltd

Printed in Singapore

Library of Congress Cataloging-in-Publication Data:
Foley, Erin.
  · Ecuador / Erin L. Foley
      p. cm.—(Cultures Of The World)
    Includes bibliographical references and index.
    ISBN 0-7614-0173-3 (Ecuador)
    ISBN 0-7614-0167-9 (Set)
    1. Ecuador—Juvenile literature. [1. Ecuador.]
I. Title. II. Series.
F3708.5.F65 1995
986.6—dc20   94–45266
                       CIP
                        AC

INTRODUCTION

ECUADOR is a country of astonishing diversity, displayed through its geography, its plant and animal life, and its inhabitants. Much of Ecuador's diversity derives from its position on the equator together with the presence of the Andes mountains, which form the country's backbone. These two factors provide for great climatic variations, from the snowcapped mountains and cold, foggy highlands, to humid, tropical lowlands and the Amazon jungle. To top it all off, the Galápagos Islands, which lie off Ecuador's coast, epitomize diversity. The islands are considered to be one of the most important biological regions in the world.

The enchantment of Ecuador is revealed through its different facets—from the misty patchwork of its tilled mountainsides to the cacophony of its Amazonian wildlife, or from the Europeanized and elegant Guayaquil businessman to the roughened peasant woman of the highlands, bundled in homespun wool with a felt hat covering her wary face.

CONTENTS

Indigenous children from
Chimborazo province.

CONTENTS

A Salasaca woman with the traditional broad-brimmed hat.

GEOGRAPHY

THE REPUBLIC OF ECUADOR straddles the earth's equator, for which it is named. Located on the western shoulder of South America, the relatively tranquil republic is wedged between its troubled neighbors, Colombia to the north and Peru to the south and east. The Pacific Ocean defines its western border, including the famed Galápagos ("gah-LAH-pah-gohs") Islands, which lie about 600 miles (1,000 km) off the coast of Ecuador. The entire area of the country is 105,037 square miles (272,045 sq km)—approximately the size of the state of Colorado.

Although it is one of the smaller countries in South America, Ecuador displays a startling degree of geographical diversity. The Andes Mountains form the backbone of the country, dividing continental Ecuador into three distinct geographical regions: the Costa, the Sierra, and the Oriente (which is also sometimes called the Amazon region). A fourth major region is created by the Galápagos Islands.

The Andes Mountains extend over 5,000 miles (8,045 km) along the western part of South America: from Venezuela at the top of the continent to Tierra del Fuego at its southern tip. The majestic mountain system includes numerous volcanoes and peaks that rise to more than 22,000 feet (6,705 m).

Opposite: **The Pastaza River flows out of the Sierra and through the Oriente.**

Left: **Patches of farmland texture the mountainsides in Cotapaxi Province in the Sierra.**

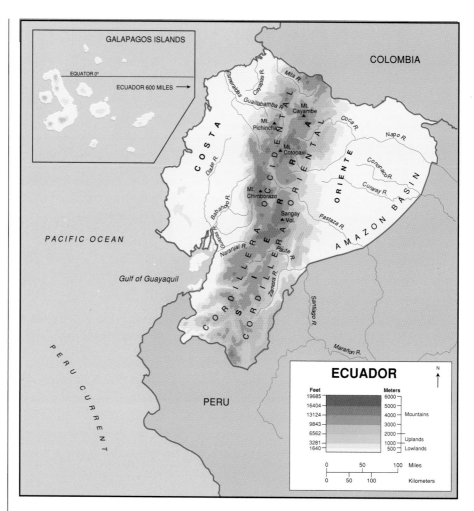

The northern Sierra constitutes an area of modern volcanism: its volcanoes stand higher and have been formed more recently. The southern Sierra is an area of ancient volcanism, where volcanoes have eroded into lower peaks.

GEOGRAPHICAL REGIONS

Differences in altitude between the various regions account for the great diversity of climates in Ecuador.

THE SIERRA Two major chains of the Andes mountains, running from north to south, form the Sierra: the Cordillera Occidental ("kor-dee-YAY-rah oak-see-dain-TAHL") and the Cordillera Oriental ("or-ee-yen-TAHL"). The Cordillera Oriental is wider, and its peaks average over 13,100 feet (4,000 m) in altitude. The Cordillera Occidental, however, includes the highest point in Ecuador—Mount Chimborazo, at 20,556 feet (6,265 m).

The Sierra includes over 30 peaks of volcanic origin, several of which are still active. The region is often subjected to powerful geological forces, such as earthquakes and tremors. The Sierra has always been more densely populated than either the Costa or the Oriente, although melting snowcaps from the volcanoes can wreak havoc on inhabitants of the Sierra by burying homes in mudslides and avalanches.

Between the Cordilleras lies a plateau rich with volcanic soil. Several mountain spurs, called *nudos* ("NOO-dohs"), cut across the plateau. The *nudos* form large, isolated basins between the Cordilleras.

The most active volcano in the Sierra is Mount Sangay, with an elevation of 18,247 feet (5,562 m). Although its last major lava outpouring was in 1946, Mount Sangay's crater constantly bubbles with lava and fire.

Mount Cotopaxi, at 19,342 feet (5,895 m) high, is the highest active volcano in the world. Cotopaxi continues to steam but has not erupted since 1877.

THE COSTA The coastal region of Ecuador consists of coastal lowlands, coastal mountains, and rolling hills separating river valleys. The widest part of the region is only 93 miles (150 km) wide, from the coast of Manabí Province to the foothills of the Andes. The narrowest part, in the southern part of Guayas Province, measures 10 miles (16 km) in width.

A coastal mountain chain, the Cordillera Costañera ("kohs-tah-NYAY-rah"), which extends from Esmeraldas in the north to Guayaquil in the south, divides the Costa into the Costa Externa ("ex-TAIR-nah") and the Costa Interna ("een-TAIR-nah"). The lowlands of the Costa Externa lie closest to the coast, while the Costa Interna lies next to the Andes. The coastal lowlands do not exceed 650 feet (200 m) in elevation; even the coastal mountains rise to less than 3,300 feet (1000 m).

THE ORIENTE Until the 1970s, the Oriente remained isolated geographically and culturally from the rest of Ecuador. After a severe drought in the Sierra, however, the government encouraged people to colonize the jungle frontier. Given incentives such as tax exemptions for businesses and land deeds for migrants, thousands of homesteaders migrated to the Oriente, arriving from Colombia and other parts of Ecuador in droves.

Together with the recent discovery and exploitation of oil reserves in northeastern Ecuador in 1967, the rapid colonization of the Oriente enormously distressed the environment and its indigenous inhabitants, forcing many of the reclusive indigenous Amazonians to retreat farther and farther into the forest.

CLIMATE AND SEASONS

The Costa experiences little seasonal variation in temperature, although it does tend to be hotter during the rainy season, especially February through April. The average coastal temperatures range from 73°F (22.5°C) in the south to 79°F (25.8°C) in the north. There is little seasonal variation except when the *El Niño* phenomenon (see box) causes drastic changes in the climate. The Costa Interna is separated from the effects of ocean currents by the Cordillera Costañera. The climate tends to be hot and humid, with

EL NIÑO

El Niño is a climatological phenomenon that occurs at irregular intervals every six or seven years. Due to a change in atmospheric pressure, the warm ocean currents that normally flow from January through April instead flow for a longer period, raising temperatures, ocean tides, and humidity. Ocean temperatures increase so much that a lot of marine life is unable to survive. By damaging the food supply at the lower end of the food chain, El Niño starves many other species, including marine iguanas and seabirds—and humans. It can cause also flooding and landslides. El Niño was particularly harsh in 1982–1983, when it caused severe problems for the fishing industry, as well as for Galápagos marine life. The picture shows stormy weather caused by El Niño in that year.

The name El Niño, which means "baby boy," derives from the fact that it usually appears around Christmas.

temperatures averaging 79°F (25.8°C). The rainy season, or winter, lasts from December through May, and is characterized by constant rainfall.

The climate of the Sierra tends to depend more on altitude than on seasonal change. The hottest month averages about 61°F (15.9°C), and the coolest month drops to about 55°F (12.6°C). Temperatures vary more through the course of the day, in fact, due to the strong sunshine and the high altitude. Mornings are often bright and sunny; the afternoons are cloudy, often with heavy downpours of rain; and the evenings can be chilly and blanketed in thick fog. The residents of Quito like to note that one can experience "all of the seasons in one day!" in the capital city.

The relatively uniform climate of the Oriente varies only slightly between the two subregions. The Eastern lowlands exemplify an equatorial climate with abundant rainfall, which sometimes measures nearly 200 inches in a year. Temperatures average 77°F (24.7°C) in the western portion. The jungle also receives high levels of rainfall and averages above 82°F (27.5°C).

The Costa is primarily influenced by the cold Peruvian Current, which cools coastal waters and causes heavy fog.

Isla Bartolomé in the Galapagos Islands. The Galápagos were formed more recently than the South American continent, by underwater volcanoes that erupted and rose to the ocean's surface. The region remains very actively volcanic.

The six small islands are all less than two square miles (5 sq km) each in area. The thirteen larger islands range from five square miles (12 sq km) to 1,789 square miles (4,633 sq km).

THE GALÁPAGOS ISLANDS

Ecuador claimed possession of the Galápagos Islands, officially known as the Archipiélago de Colón, in 1832. Named for the giant tortoises that inhabit the islands, the archipelago consists of more than 19 islands and islets. The entire land mass of the Galápagos is 3,074 square miles (7,961 sq km), located about 700 miles (1126 km) west of the coast of Ecuador. At 75 miles (120 km) long, the largest island, Isabela, constitutes more than half of that area. It also contains the highest mountain peak, Santo Tomás, at 4,887 feet (1,489 m). Numerous small islets dot the archipelago.

DARWIN AND THE GALÁPAGOS

Charles Darwin was just beginning to develop his theory of evolution when he visited the Galápagos Islands in 1835. Not only did Galápagos species differ from their relatives on the mainland of South America, but they also differed from one island to another. Migrant species from the mainland settled in the new environment, where they gradually adapted to their habitat. In noting that each original species had thus evolved into one or more separate species, Darwin developed the theory of "natural selection."

PLANTS AND ANIMALS OF THE GALÁPAGOS

Bird species populate the island most visibly. There are 58 resident bird species on the Galápagos, plus about 30 migrant species. Of the resident species, 28 are endemic, meaning that they do not breed anywhere else in the world. The most well-known Galápagos birds include the blue-footed booby (shown below), the Galápagos penguin (the most northerly penguin in the world), the red-footed booby, frigatebirds (which exhibit a spectacular courtship display), flamingos, and of course, Darwin's finches.

Mammals had a more difficult time in migrating to the Galápagos because of the distance. Thus, only six mammal species are endemic to the islands: two seals, two bats, and two species of rice rats. Other mammals include feral goats, pigs, burros, cats, dogs, rats, and mice.

People inhabit only five of the islands, constituting in 1991 a growing population of about 14,000. They make a living primarily from tourism, fishing, and farming. More than half of the residents live in the city of Puerto Ayora on Isla Santa Cruz, which is the second largest island. Relatively few small land mammals and insects inhabit the islands, but larger land mammals have become common because settlers brought their domesticated livestock with them.

Twenty-two reptile species inhabit the islands, 19 of which are endemic. These include tortoises, or *galápagos* (shown above), marine turtles, the ubiquitous iguanas and lizards, geckos, and three species of snakes, all of which are nonpoisonous constrictors.

Galápagos waters swarm with more than 307 species of tropical fish, at least 50 of which are native. In addition to parrotfish, angelfish, and pufferfish, several species of sharks and rays glide

through the warm waters. Many invertebrates populate the Galápagos waters and beaches, including crabs, sponges, octopuses, starfish, sea urchins, and sea cucumbers.

Approximately 1,300 species of plants have been recorded in the Galápagos. They are spread out among six different zones of vegetation. These vary, on the larger islands, from arid desert environments to the lush tropical vegetation of the highlands.

The most striking plant of the *páramo* ("PAH-rah-moh"), or highlands, is the *frailejón* ("fry-YON"), meaning "grey friar." As tall as an adult human, they sometimes appear to float in the páramo mist.

Opposite: The most common Andes animal is the domestic *llama* ("YA-mah").

The mangrove is a spindly tree with intertwined stilt-like roots that secure it in sandy soil. The tree has developed the remarkable ability to grow in salt water. Its spreading roots provide shelter for many species of fish and invertebrates, and its branches provide nesting habitats for pelicans and other seabirds.

FLORA AND FAUNA

Due to the great variety of habitats within its small territory, ecologists consider Ecuador to be one of the most species-rich countries in the world.

COSTA Ecuador's coast is covered with lush tropical vegetation. The northern corner above Esmeraldas and the southeastern corner of the Costa consist of tropical rainforest. Flora includes trees, lianas (climbing vines), and epiphytes (plants that take all of their moisture and some of their nutrients from the humid air). In the Guayas River valley, the forest contains balsa, which is exploited for use as a light lumber.

The vegetation between Esmeraldas and the Gulf of Guayaquil is characterized by dry forests of deciduous and semideciduous trees, which lose their leaves during the dry season.

Thick mangrove forests once covered the swampy coast and the river floodplains. Most of the mangroves, however, have been cleared away for the production of shrimp—thus endangering the breeding grounds of many animal species.

SIERRA Most of the native highland vegetation has been replaced by agricultural crops or altered by periodic burning. The valleys, or *hoyas*, are covered with thorny woodlands, which change to low evergreen forests at the edges. At the higher elevations in the more isolated valleys can be found the tropical cloud forests. In these rare environments trapped clouds drench the forest with a fine mist, nourishing a variety of plants, such as ferns, orchids, and other epiphytes, and such rare animals as the woolly tapir, the Andean spectacled bear, and the puma.

The highland area above 11,500 feet (3,500 m) is known as the *páramo*; its bleak environment supports little more than hard bunchgrasses and small herbaceous plants. The Andean condor is an endangered species. It has a wing span of nearly 10 feet (3 m).

ORIENTE The Oriente consists primarily of tropical rainforest with vegetation similar to the Costa. A wide variety of monkeys inhabit the rainforest, as well as sloths, jaguars, ocelots, and smaller carnivores. The rainforest also contains several hoofed animals, including the tapir, deer, and peccary (a relative of the pig, covered with long, dark bristles). Many of these mammals serve as a source of food for the Oriente peoples.

A wide variety of parrots and toucans also populate the rainforest, as does the large harpy eagle, which is capable of snatching monkeys and sloths off trees as it flies by. Approximately 1,000 species of fish have been recorded, including the electric eel and the piranha.

Over 400 species of amphibians and 400 species of reptiles live in Ecuador. Some of the more exotic frogs include marsupial frogs, which carry their eggs and hatched tadpoles in pouches under their skins, and poison-arrow frogs, whose skin glands exude toxins strong enough to cause paralysis and death in animals and humans. Indigenous forest dwellers use these toxins as a poison for the tips of their hunting arrows.

Well over 20,000 species of plants have been recorded in Ecuador, and new species are discovered every year. In comparison, the entire continent of North America holds only some 17,000 species.

15

Quito was long known as the "monastery of Latin America" because of its tranquility and religious conservatism. Today, however, it is a bustling capital.

RIVERS

Ecuador's rivers generally rise in the Sierra and flow either east toward the Amazon or west toward the Pacific Ocean. They originate either from melted snow at the edges of the mountain snowcaps or from the heavy rains that occur at higher elevations.

Two major river systems drain the Costa: the Guayas and the Esmeraldas. Nearly 40 miles (64 km) in length, the Guayas River forms at the juncture of the Daule and Babahoyo Rivers, north of Guayaquil. The Esmeraldas river system originates in the Sierra as the Guayllabamba River. It flows west out of the Sierra for nearly 200 miles (320 km), emptying into the Pacific Ocean near the town of Esmeraldas.

The major rivers of the Oriente include the Pastaza, the Napo, and the Putumayo. The Pastaza is formed by the confluence of the Chambo and Petate Rivers, which flow out of the Sierra. The Pastaza includes the 200-foot (320 km) Agoyán waterfall. The Napo River rises near Mt. Cotopaxi and ranges in width from 1,640 feet (499 m) to well over a mile (1.6 km) wide. The Napo is the primary river used for transport in the Eastern lowlands. The Putumayo forms part of the border with Colombia.

CITIES

More than half of all Ecuadorians now live in cities. Regional rivalries are intense between the Sierra and the Costa, and animosities center on the respective regional urban centers, Quito and Guayaquil.

The residents of each urban center feel great pride in their own city and despise the other. Quiteños disparage the people of Guayaquil as being uncouth, sacrilegious, and lazy, and lacking in ambition and culture. Costeños in general laugh off the criticism and even embrace it as an accurate characterization. Guayaquil is the economic capital of the country, and residents feel that, although they produce the money, it ends up in the government coffers in Quito.

QUITO Ecuador's capital is the second-largest city, with a population of 1,100,000. Quito is located in the northern part of the Sierra, and the site has been inhabited since pre-Columbian times. It is a very old and beautiful city, with a mixture of colonial and modern architecture. Until the oil boom in the 1970s, cultural life centered in the colonial part of the city, with its narrow cobblestone streets and 400-year-old architecture. In 1978, UNESCO declared Quito's colonial center to be one of the world's cultural heritage sites.

GUAYAQUIL Guayaquil is the most populous city in the country and the economic center of Ecuador. Some 1,500,000 people live there in crowded, hot, and humid conditions. Yet they pride themselves on their easy-going lifestyle and their irreverent sense of humor. People seem to respond to the heat with accelerated gaiety, and the streets are in constant motion with cars, taxis, buses, street vendors, and pedestrians.

The city is overcrowded and continues to grow as farmers and agricultural workers from the countryside seek greater economic opportunities in the urban areas. The rural-urban migration has led to the formation of large shantytowns, which generally have no electricity or even sewage facilities.

A street in downtown Guayaquil. Guayas Province takes its name from the chief of the Punás, who courageously resisted conquest by both the Incas and the Spanish. Legends say that he killed his wife, Quill, before drowning himself in order to prevent the Spanish from capturing them. Guayaquil is named after the couple.

17

HISTORY

ECUADOR CONTAINS ONE OF THE MOST DIVERSE indigenous cultures in Latin America. Many contemporary peoples—such as the Salasaca, the Saraguro, the Otavalo, and the peoples of the Oriente—trace their roots back to the Incas and before. The history of Ecuador begins with them.

Archaeologists have discovered in Ecuador the most ancient ceramic artifacts in all of the Americas. The oldest ceramics date back to 3500 B.C., belonging to the Valdivia culture (4800–1200 B.C.), which rose and expanded along the coast, near the present-day province of Manabí. The culture displayed advanced social organization, agricultural knowledge, and artistic expression. They produced ceramics of extraordinary beauty.

Most of the major archeological sites in Ecuador produce more recent artifacts, from the last 2,000 years. Another major pre-Colombian culture was the Tolita (A.D. 1200-1522), which in addition to producing beautifully crafted ceramics, also worked with gold and even platinum, a metal not discovered in Europe until the mid-1800s.

By the 13th century, Ecuador was populated by many different indigenous cultures. These people were primarily sedentary farmers; they grew such crops as corn, quinoa, beans, many types of squash, and more than 320 types of potatoes. They resided primarily on the mountainsides and in the valleys, in widely scattered villages.

Opposite: **Ingapirca marked a high point of civilization in the area that is now Ecuador.**

Above: **A pre-Colombian figure shows the vitality of the Inca culture.**

BIRTHPLACE OF SOUTH AMERICAN CIVILIZATION?

Ecuador contains a vast and varied wealth of archeological remains from different time periods. Archeologists have discovered ancient trade links between the Valdivia coastal culture, the Sierra, and Central America. They speculate that the Valdivia culture might even have been related to ancient Asian cultures. Valdivia ceramics show marked resemblance to ancient Japanese pottery from the Jomon culture.

The architectural mastery of the Incas is evident in the ancient city of Ingapirca and, on a much larger scale, in Machu Picchu, the Inca capital in the mountains of Peru.

Opposite: **The likeness of Atahualpa peers out of the cliffs in Cañar Province.**

THE INCA EMPIRE

The Inca civilization was the most advanced civilization in pre-Colombian South America. Their culture was organized as a hierarchy headed by the Inca, who was their god in human form. The Andean empire, called Tawantinsuyu, was centered in modern-day Peru but extended into Chile, Bolivia, and Ecuador. In 1463, the Incas moved northward through the Sierra and defeated the Quitu. The 11th Inca, Huayna Cápac, finally subdued the population around the Gulf of Guayaquil and the island of Puná. With this expedition, the Inca annexed all of present-day Ecuador.

Huayna Cápac ruled through the local chiefs as long as they were willing to accept the divine authority of the Inca and pay tribute to the empire. If he met any resistance, he would send large groups of the local population to distant areas of the Inca empire, replacing them with colonists from as far away as modern-day Bolivia and Chile. Thus, he spread the Inca language, Quechua, throughout the new territory. The Salasaca and Saraguro Indians of present-day Ecuador are descendants of such relocated Inca colonists.

CONQUEST OF THE INCAS

Huayna Cápac liked Ecuador so much that he made Quito into the secondary capital of the empire and lived there until his sudden death in 1527. The death of Huayna Cápac by an unknown disease (possibly carried by the Europeans, who were already making their way south from Mexico) sparked a civil war between his two sons, Atahualpa and Huáscar. Huáscar was defeated by Atahualpa and the Ecuadorian Incas only days before the Spaniards arrived in Ecuador.

Francisco Pizarro was one of many illiterate adventurers who joined the conquest seeking riches for Spain and especially for themselves. Pizarro landed on the coast of Ecuador in 1531 but waited until September 24, 1532 to march south. He encountered Atahualpa, the new Inca, almost by coincidence. Atahualpa was resting near Cajamarca, following the defeat and capture of his brother Huáscar. He had known of the arrival of the Europeans for months but did not seem to feel threatened by them. Perhaps he felt so secure in his own invincible divinity as Inca that he felt no fear; or perhaps he assumed that his forces, which far outnumbered Pizarro's, could easily defeat the Europeans.

Pizarro summoned Atahualpa for a meeting. Atahualpa responded in the company of several thousand of his best troops. The Spanish chaplain who accompanied Pizarro called upon Atahualpa to submit to the Spanish crown and to the Christian god. Atahualpa responded disparagingly and threw the Christian prayer book on the ground—at which point concealed Spanish soldiers opened fire. They killed thousands in the immediate bloodbath and took Atahualpa captive on November 16, 1532.

Pizarro held Atahualpa in prison for several months, demanding ransom in return for the Inca's freedom. Despite a promise to free Atahualpa, he ordered the Inca to be hanged on August 29, 1533.

Potatoes were introduced to Europe and the rest of the world by the Andean natives. The starchy tuber became an essential part of the diet all over the world because it was cheap, nutritious, and easy to grow.

21

Isabel Godin des Odonais was lost in the Amazon in 1769 and spent 19 years with natives there.

COLONIAL RULE

The Inca civilization was so well organized that the Spanish simply took the Inca's place. They continued to gather tribute from the Inca subjects in the form of goods and labor. Only the Sierra natives were successfully subjugated by the Spanish, and rebellions continued to erupt throughout the 16th century. Nearly one-fourth of the native population escaped domination by fleeing to the jungles of the Oriente and Esmeraldas. There they remained unconquered throughout the 16th and 17th centuries.

The Spanish created a "New World" replica of the European feudal system. They had enormous resources to exploit and an abundant supply of labor. The adventurers transformed themselves into feudal overlords; whatever their position in Spain, they became landed elite in America. The Sierra remained isolated from the rest of the world for the 300 years of colonial rule.

The natives were forced to work as laborers. They had few rights and little protection from abuse. Ecuador's indigenous population at the time of the conquest was somewhere between 750,000 to 1 million. The coastal population was almost exterminated by European diseases within a century.

African slaves were extremely expensive in comparison to the nearly free labor of the indebted Indians. The African slaves were used to work on the hot and humid coastal plantations where the Serrano peoples were unable to adapt. By the end of the colonial period, approximately 60,000 people of African descent lived in Ecuador.

INDEPENDENCE

Ecuador's battle for independence started with increasing civil disturbances in the Sierra in the mid-1700s, beginning with the 1765 tax revolt in Quito. This was followed by a series of native rebellions in Latacunga and Riobamba.

In 1808, Napoleon Bonaparte placed his brother Joseph on the Spanish throne. Spanish citizens living in Ecuador resented the action and organized local action groups loyal to the Spanish King Ferdinand VII. In October 1820, a local *junta* ("HOON-tah") declared independence in Guayaquil, led by the poet José Joaquín Olmedo. The rebels appealed to independence movements in Venezuela and Argentina. Both countries responded promptly with troops. "The Great Liberator" Simon Bolívar was aided by his lieutenant Antonio José de Sucre Alcalá and the Argentine José de San Martín. Together their forces won the decisive Battle of Pichincha against the Spanish on May 24, 1822.

Two months after the Battle of Pichincha, Simón Bolívar was received by Quito with a hero's welcome. Ecuador joined the Confederation of Gran Colombia, which included present-day Venezuela and Colombia. For the next several years, Ecuador, as the District of the South, was on the front lines of a war against Spanish forces in Peru. Growing separatist tendencies within the Confederation finally persuaded separatists in Quito to dissolve their union with Gran Colombia in May 1830. By August, a constituent assembly had drawn up a constitution for the new country, which they named the Republic of Ecuador because of its position on the equator.

Simón Bolivar, while dying from tuberculosis, expressed his heartbreak over the dissolution of Gran Colombia and the futility of his struggle: "America is ungovernable. Those who have served the revolution have plowed the sea."

In 1990, the National Confederation of Indigenous Nationalities of Ecuador (CONAIE) organized an uprising throughout the Sierra. The indigenous rebels demanded the return of traditional community-held lands, recognition of Quechua as an official language, and compensation for environmental damage caused by the petroleum companies.

The caudillo *("cow-DEE-yoh") is "the man with a mission," that is, a man who believes that he is indispensable to the task of "saving the country." He is charismatic, reasonably intelligent, and he commands both attention and respect. Once voted into office, the caudillo often assumes almost dictatorial powers; for this reason, he has been described as "the monarch in republican dress."*

CONSTITUTIONS AND CAUDILLOS

The new country was plagued by instability as the political elites fought among themselves through the first 30 years of independence. Between 1830 and 1925, the country was governed by 40 different regimes. Between 1830 and 1860, liberal and conservative caudillos vied for power through unconstitutional seizures of power.

The rivalry between Quito and Guayaquil, which was to characterize Ecuadorian politics for at least the next 150 years, was becoming more pronounced. Quito was the home of the politically and religiously conservative, landed elite, who resisted change and depended on the indigenous labor force to work its large estates. Guayaquil had developed into a cosmopolitan, bustling seaport whose liberals supported free enterprise, minority rights, and anticlericalism.

From 1860-1895, the conservatives controlled the government, most notably through Gabriel García Moreno, who ruled the country from 1860-1875. The Liberal Party ruled the country from 1895-1925, led by General José Eloy Alfaro Delgado, a popular caudillo. The period from 1925 to 1948 was marked by economic crisis, political instability, and civil unrest. A total

VELASCO IBARRA

Between 1931 and 1944, five out of six presidents were overthrown or forced to resign from office. In 1944, one of these men was reappointed as president by the military. This was the second of five presidencies for José María Velasco Ibarra, who dominated the post-World War II period and who epitomizes the Ecuadorian caudillo.

Velasco Ibarra was a dynamic populist who appealed to the voters by promising social justice and punishment for the corrupt Liberal oligarchy. Although his base of support was among the Conservatives, he strongly appealed to "the common man." He switched his political positions as suited his purpose. He was such a charismatic figure that he was elected president five times, and yet so objectionable that he actually completed only one of his five presidential terms. He was overthrown for the last time in 1972.

of 22 heads of state governed the country during this period, and only one successfully completed his term.

On July 5, 1941 Peru invaded Ecuador, thus bringing to a head the border conflict that had broken out intermittently since independence. Peru occupied Ecuador until January 1942, when both countries signed the Protocol of Peace, Friendship, and Boundaries, also known as the Río Protocol. In this treaty, Ecuador renounced its claim to almost half its territory, approximately 78,000 square miles of its Amazonian region, which outraged Ecuadorians and resulted in a resurgence of nationalism. Many Ecuadorians to this day have not accepted the protocol, and the Ecuadorian map still includes the disputed territory.

Repeated attempts at land reform failed to solve Ecuador's ethnic disputes. In May 1990, 1,000 indigenous people marched into Quito, demanding recognition of their land rights. In April 1992, several thousand people from the Oriente marched to Quito demanding official recognition of the historical rights to their lands. President Rodrigo Borja granted them legal title to more than 2,500,000 acres (1,000,000 hectares) of land.

President Sixto Durán Ballén was elected in May 1992; within six months he announced a program of austerity measures to curb inflation and lower the deficit. The economic program ignited strikes, violent demonstrations, and bomb attacks in Quito and Guayaquil.

GOVERNMENT

THE REPUBLIC OF ECUADOR has a long history of political instability. A rapid succession of presidents and new constitutions whirled through the first century of the republic, and dictatorships became common in the middle of the 20th century. A total of 87 governments have changed hands in Ecuador's 165 years of independent rule, averaging out to less than two years of power per regime. Only 21 of those governments resulted from popular elections, and many of the elections were fraudulent. Political instability is also reflected in the numerous constitutions since the Republic declared itself an independent country in 1822.

Although Ecuador has managed to avoid large-scale uprisings and guerrilla wars, the country remains an immature democracy, beset by continuing political contests and economic crises. Nonetheless, Ecuador's fledgling democracy has survived since 1979.

Ecuadorians like to joke that whereas many Latin American countries have suffered under dictaduras *("deek-tah-DOO-rahs"), or dictatorships, Ecuador has been subjected to mere* dictablandas *("deek-tah-BLAHN-dahs")— making a play on the words* dura *(hard) and* blanda *(weak).*

Opposite: **A police officer in Quito.**

Left: **Paratroopers in transit. Ecuador maintains a reputation for relative tranquility, especially, as Ecuadorians like to point out, in comparison to its neighbors, Colombia and Peru.**

NATIONAL GOVERNMENT

Ecuador is a democratic state headed by a president. All Ecuadorians between the ages of 18 and 75 are required to vote unless they are disabled or sick, absent from the country, or otherwise incapacitated. They must directly elect the president and vice-president by an absolute majority, which usually requires a second round of elections.

EXECUTIVE BRANCH The executive branch consists of the president, the vice-president, the ministers of state and their subordinate officials, and the National Development Council (Conade). The president serves a four-year term and may not run for reelection.

Conade determines the general economic and social policies of the state and prepares development plans for approval by the president. The body is composed of the vice-president, four ministers, the president of the Monetary Board, and one representative each of congress, the mayors, the provincial prefects, organized labor, the commercial associations, and the polytechnical universities and schools.

THE 1979 CONSTITUTION

The 1979 constitution provides the foundation for the current democratic period. It grants full citizenship and voting rights to all Ecuadorians over 18 years of age, for the first time including illiterate people. It prohibits discrimination based on race, sex, religion, language, or social status. It also creates a unicameral congress and four legislative commissions and requires candidates in popular elections to affiliate with a legally recognized party. Amendments to the 1979 constitution limited the presidential term to four years, without possibility of reelection.

LEGISLATIVE BRANCH Although most previous constitutions established bicameral legislatures, the 1979 constitution provides for a unicameral legislature, known as the Chamber of Deputies, or Congress. Congress holds the power to interpret the constitution and enact legislation.

Congress appoints several high-ranking public officials, including the supreme court justices. The legislature may dismiss members of the president's cabinet. The Congress may prosecute the president and vice-president, as well as other public officials.

There are two classes of deputies in the congress, national and provincial representatives. Twelve national deputies are elected for a four-year term, whereas provincial deputies, elected according to proportional representation, serve a two-year term.

The Chamber of Deputies meets once a year, from August 10 through October 8. When necessary, the legislature may call an extraordinary session.

JUDICIAL BRANCH The judiciary consists of three organs of equal status and importance: the Supreme Court of Justice, the Fiscal Tribunal, and the Contentious Administrative Tribunal. The Supreme Court of Justice supervises the superior, lower, and special courts.

The Supreme Court of Justice has only a secondary role in interpreting the constitution, although it may initiate constitutional reform. Any of the three judicial organs may declare a law unconstitutional, but their ruling must be reviewed by the Supreme Court of Justice.

The Tribunal of Constitutional Guarantees interprets and enforces compliance with the constitution. Although it may suspend unconstitutional laws, it must submit its ruling to the congress for final approval.

Above: **Riot police at a demonstration in Cuenca.**

Opposite: **An election poster for a Liberal candidate.**

MILITARY AND POLICE

The military establishment has historically played an important role, whether directly or indirectly, in Ecuadorian politics. Unlike the armed forces in most Latin American countries, which tend to ally themselves with the elite, landowning class, the Ecuadorian military early on identified itself with the merchant class and with the Liberal Party. Thus, the military has historically viewed itself as an agent of progressive change.

However progressive and mild the military dictators of Ecuador have been, they nonetheless governed unconstitutionally, from their seizure of power to their abuse of human rights. Although the 1979 constitution defines the armed forces as nonpolitical and as an instrument of civil authority, the military continues to exert an influence over the political process. After the 1979 transition to democracy, the military prohibited any investigation into human rights issues by President Jaime Roldós.

Also in contrast to many Latin American military forces, the Ecuadorian military focuses more, though not exclusively, on national security from external threats than it does on guarding internal security from civil disorder. The primary concern of the military continues to be the perceived threat posed by Peru along their shared Amazonian border. The Ecuadorian military was twice defeated in conflict with the better-equipped Peruvian military, in 1941 and 1981. The armed forces also remain alert to infiltrations from drug traffickers and armed rebels from Colombia along Ecuador's northern boundary.

POLITICAL PARTIES

Ecuadorian politics have traditionally been controlled by the rival Conservative Party (PC) and Radical Liberal Party (PLR). Centered in the Sierra, the Conservative Party advocates a strong, centralized government, close cooperation between the Roman Catholic Church and the state, and the preservation of private property. The Radical Liberal Party, generally known as the Liberals, has suffered from a great deal of factionalism. Centered in the Costa, the Liberals generally emphasize anticlericalism and agrarian reform.

Although personalistic caudillo rule has always characterized Ecuadorian politics more than party politics, candidates for election must now affiliate themselves with a legally recognized party. Contemporary parties span the political spectrum from communist, Maoist, and socialist, to Christian Democratic, Social Democratic, and even quasi-fascist parties, such as the Ecuadorian Nationalist Revolutionary Action (ARNE), which became the ruling party when Febres Cordero assumed the presidency in 1984.

ECONOMY

ECUADOR HAS LONG DEPENDED on the wealth of a single export, making its economy vulnerable to "boom-and-bust" economic cycles as the price of its major export rises and falls on the world market. During the 19th century, Ecuador was one of the leading producers of cocoa. By the 1930s, the cocoa industry had "gone bust," declining due to disease and foreign competition. In 1947, bananas replaced cocoa as Ecuador's primary export. The "banana boom" lasted for less than a decade, and then Ecuador's economy floundered until petroleum was discovered in the Oriente in 1967. As an oil-exporting country, Ecuador enjoyed enormous new wealth for about 10 years. When the price of oil dropped in the 1980s, however, Ecuador was plunged into another economic crisis, exacerbated by the need to pay interest on large foreign debts.

Petroleum remains Ecuador's primary source of export earnings, and agriculture and fishing continue to be an important sector of the economy. The service industry, however, is the fastest-growing economic sector and employs nearly half of the work force.

Although the 1992 Gross National Product was over $11.8 billion, Ecuador has not yet completely recovered from the debt crisis of the early 1980s. The Gross Domestic Product (GDP) has increased annually, but Ecuador still has one of the lowest per capita GDPs in South America, equivalent to $1,070 per person.

Opposite: **Oil drilling in the Oriente.**

Left: **A casava field with banana trees in the Costa.**

AGRICULTURE

Agriculture employed approximately 28.8% of the labor force in 1992 and constituted an estimated 20% of the GDP. Bananas remain the country's leading export crop, followed by coffee and cocoa. Nearly four million tons were produced in 1992, making Ecuador the world's largest exporter of bananas. Bananas are produced on large plantations in the Costa.

Coffee is the second most valuable agricultural export. Ecuador produces both the arabica and robusta varieties, cultivating them primarily in the hills of Manabí Province and in the western foothills of the Andes, south of Guayaquil. In 1992, approximately 197,700 tons were produced, most of which was processed and exported. Unlike bananas, coffee is usually grown on small landholdings.

Cocoa was once the basis of Ecuador's export agriculture, but the industry was nearly wiped out in the 1920s by a fungal disease. New disease-resistant varieties have revitalized cocoa production since the end of World War II, however. Sugar was an important export crop in the 1960s and 1970s, but in the 1980s Ecuador actually had to import refined sugar. Farmers also cultivate cotton, hemp, tea, tobacco, and a large variety of minor fruit and vegetable crops.

LIVESTOCK Ecuadorians tend to raise livestock on small landholdings, primarily for domestic consumption. The Costa and Oriente produce mainly beef cattle, grazing them on land otherwise unsuitable for agriculture; the Serranos raise dairy cattle and graze them in the fertile valleys. Many Ecuadorians also raise pigs, sheep, goats, and poultry.

FISHING Ecuador's ocean border provides a rich resource for coastal residents, and fisheries have become one of the fastest growing industries in Ecuador. In 1986, Ecuador became the world's largest shrimp exporter, producing 118,900 tons in 1991. Shrimp production has increased enormously in recent years due to the proliferation of shrimp farms in the warm coastal waters, especially in the Gulf of Guayaquil, where the extensive shrimp farms are fast replacing native mangrove trees.

Tuna represents the most important saltwater fish for the fishing industry. Ecuador modernized its tuna fleet in the 1980s to include refrigerated boats and leased several large nets from the United States.

FORESTRY Although forest covers approximately 50% of Ecuador, forestry only contributes about four percent to the GDP. Ecuador is one of the world's leading exporters of balsawood. Many Ecuadorians use the forests as a source of fuel and for construction in rural areas. Other products are obtained from Ecuador's trees, such as quinine from cinchona bark, buttons from ivory palm nuts, and mattress stuffing from the silky kapok of the ceiba (silk-cotton) tree.

Top: **Fishing in Guayaquil.**

Bottom: **Ecuador's extensive forests yield valuable hardwoods.**

Opposite: **Women carrying corn. Food crops produced for domestic consumption include sugarcane, rice, barley, corn, and wheat.**

The Trans-Ecuadorian Pipeline snakes across some hills.

The indigenous peoples of the Oriente resent the invasion of their traditional territory by the oil companies. Many refer to petroleum as "excrement of the devil," because of the way that its exploitation has altered and even destroyed their environment.

PETROLEUM AND MINING

Ecuador began exploring for oil in the Oriente in the 1920s, but didn't strike it rich until 1967, when several abundant oil fields were discovered near Lago Agrio (officially known as Nueva Loja). Oil companies moved quickly to exploit the reserves, establishing over 50 new oil wells within the next 20 years.

Ecuador constructed the Trans-Ecuadorian Pipeline to carry crude petroleum 312 miles (502 km) across the Andes from the Oriente to a refinery south of Esmeraldas. An earthquake in March 1987 caused a landslide that destroyed about 25 miles (40 km) of the pipeline near Quito.

Unlike many oil-exporting countries, Ecuador refines less than 50% of its petroleum, preventing the country from receiving the full potential value of this resource. Petroleum production totaled approximately 1.9 billion barrels in 1991 and constituted over 14% of the 1992 GDP.

Mining contributed only six percent to the GDP in 1990 and generally plays a relatively small role in the economy. Mining employs only about 7,000 people, primarily in the extraction of limestone. Next to petroleum, however, Ecuador's most valuable extracted resource is gold. In 1990, Ecuador exported more than 11 tons of gold, primarily extracted from remote gold districts in the southern Sierra.

Other minerals, such as silver, copper, zinc, uranium, lead, sulfur, and kaolin, are mined in smaller quantities. Ecuador also has large resources of natural gas, which remain largely unexploited.

MANUFACTURING

Manufacturing accounted for approximately 17% of the GDP in 1992, concentrated primarily in textiles and food processing. The manufacturing sector consists of a greater percentage of small producers than do the other economic sectors. Of the 35,000 industrial establishments existing in the early 1980s, only 28 employed more than 500 workers. More than 31,000 firms each employed fewer than five people. The primary occupations include textile manufacturing, food processing, shoemaking, woodworking, and furniture making.

Two-thirds of the country's factories are located in Guayaquil or Quito. The primary industries in Guayaquil include agricultural and beverage processing plants, sawmills, shipyards, iron foundries, and cement and chemical plants. Quito's major industries consist of textile production and food processing.

The food processing industries consist primarily of sugar refineries, rice mills, and flour mills. Mills in the Costa process rice and sugar, whereas flour is processed throughout the Sierra. The textile industry, also centered in the Sierra, is characterized by small factories, many of which started from home weaving businesses.

A manager counts money at an Ecuadorian gold mine.

37

Loading bananas on a ship for export.

SERVICE INDUSTRY

The service industry contributed 44.7% of the GDP in 1992, constituting the largest part of Ecuador's economy. A full 46% of the labor force worked in the service sector in 1990. The largest components of the service industry are wholesale and retail trade, financial services, transportation, and communications.

Tourism plays a relatively minor role in Ecuador's economy. In 1985, approximately 250,000 tourists visited Ecuador, primarily from Colombia, the United States, and Western Europe.

TRANSPORTATION Buses and cars provide the primary means of transportation, traveling through the countryside on gravel or dirt roads, or along the twisting, hairpin turns of Ecuador's highway system. Although many roads become impassable during the rainy season, the major urban centers are connected by all-weather asphalt highways. The Pan-American Highway is the principal highway of Ecuador, following the route of the Inca imperial highway through the Sierra. Four paved highways connect it to the north-south coastal highway.

Railroads were once the primary means of travel within the regions and between the Sierra and the Costa, but the rail system has declined in importance since the 1950s. Air transport has been developed in recent decades, with 179 airports throughout the country. Ecuador has four major airlines, one of which offers both domestic and international service.

Ecuador's waterways serve as transport routes for foreign trade, especially along the coast. Guayaquil is the country's main port. Riverboats and canoes navigate the rivers of the Oriente, serving as the traditional means of transport to towns and farming areas not reached by roads.

COMMUNICATIONS Despite improvements made in recent years, telecommunications services remain concentrated in Quito and Guayaquil, which hold over three-quarters of the telephones. Most of the rural areas have at most a single public telephone.

Ecuadorians in all areas of the country receive radio reception from at least one broadcasting station. Those in the major urban areas can tune into several dozen stations. Fewer people are able to watch television. Ecuador has 10 television stations, which broadcast primarily to the larger cities. Likewise, the newspaper presses are concentrated in Quito and Guayaquil, with four daily newspapers serving each city. *El Universo*, published in Guayaquil, has the largest circulation. *El Comercio*, published in Quito, is a conservative business paper with the second-largest circulation.

Top: **Public transportation in Quito.**

Bottom: **A market in Cotopaxi Province.**

39

ECUADORIANS

ECUADOR IS ONE OF THE MOST culturally diverse countries in South America, its inhabitants differentiated by ethnicity, language, region of origin, and socio-economic standing. Broad ethnic groupings include the indigenous populations, blacks, *mestizos* ("mais-TEE-sohs," persons of mixed Hispanic and indigenous parentage), Hispanics, and immigrants.

Ecuadorian society can be described as a hierarchical pyramid in which social and economic standing is directly related to ethnicity. The hierarchy is composed of a small, privileged, Hispanic elite at the top; a more numerous, politically active mestizo middle class; and a mass of poor *campesinos* ("kam-pay-SEE-nohs," or peasants), artisans, and wage earners on the bottom. Although black Ecuadorians are also pushed to the lower ranks of this hierarchy, no ethnic group is placed lower than the indigenous peoples.

There are many Ecuadorians of mixed parentage, and distinctions become somewhat blurred. During the colonial period, the term *mestizo* referred only to individuals with indigenous and Hispanic parents. Someone born of indigenous and mestizo parents was termed a *cholo* ("cho-loh"). Today, the distinction is blurred, but *cholo* is used often to describe a hierarchical category between indigenous and mestizo.

The official census does not record ethnic affiliation, but Ecuadorian society is composed of an estimated 40% indigenous peoples, 40% mestizos, 10–15% Hispanics, and approximately 5% blacks. People are identified with a particular ethnic group according to several characteristics, including physical appearance, dress, language, community membership, and self-identification.

Opposite: **A man from Salasaca province.**

Above: **Children from the Chota Valley.**

41

An indigenous tailor at Latacunga market.

THE INDIGENOUS—A SEPARATE LIFE

Hispanic and mestizo Ecuadorians refer to the indigenous peoples as *los indios* ("IHN-dyohs") or *los naturales* ("nah-tyur-AHL-ays"). Because of the pejorative associations with these names, the indigenous peoples prefer to call themselves collectively *los indígenas* ("een-DEE-hay-nahs"), which means "the indigenous ones." The individual names by which each tribe identifies itself—such as Waorani, Shuar, or Runa—mean "people." They have no word in their own vocabularies that translates into *indios* or indigenous.

Placed at the bottom of the social hierarchy, the majority of indigenous Ecuadorians see limited opportunities for economic security or social advancement unless they choose to assimilate Western values and change their ethnic affiliation by joining the mestizo community.

The indígenas are generally stigmatized by the rest of Ecuadorian society as being inferior. It is not uncommon for Serranos to refer to the indigenous peoples of the Sierra as *indios brutos*, or "beastly Indians." This perception is not diminished by the fact that many indígenas are poor and often illiterate. On the other hand, their position in society is reinforced by their limited access to education, middle-income jobs, and other social and economic opportunities that the higher classes often take for granted.

In recent years, indigenous Ecuadorians actively have begun to resist assimilation into Hispanic culture. Since the early 1980s, ethnic pride and consciousness has begun to take shape, empowering the indígenas to push for autonomous rights, recognition of Quechua as an official language, and control of their traditional lands. By increasing the number of Quechua teachers in the schools and the number of literacy programs, indigenous Ecuadorians are beginning to reinforce ethnic identity and pride. These moves have encouraged many educated indígenas to return to their native villages instead of moving away and becoming mestizo.

The indígenas have also begun to organize politically across ethnic boundaries, despite traditional cultural and geographical boundaries. The Confederation of Indigenous Nationalities of Ecuador (CONAIE) is the first federation in South America to unite Serrano and Amazonian peoples.

REGIONAL GROUPS

An incredibly diverse number of indigenous groups live scattered throughout the territory of Ecuador. Indigenous Ecuadorians differentiate themselves according to tribal and local groups. Traditionally, they distinguish themselves by hairstyle, dress, language, and even behavior.

COSTA The indigenous populations of the Costa have declined in recent decades, primarily due to westernization and migration of their members. The Colorado, the Cayapa, and the Coaiquer are the most notable indigenous groups of the region but numbered only about 4,000 members in the late 1980s. Many continue to wear traditional dress for festivals and for outsiders but wear Western clothes in their everyday life. The Cayapa and the Colorado speak different dialects of the Chibcha language, but the Coaiquer speak an entirely separate language. Migration has greatly changed the indigenous composition of the Costa: more Sierra peoples than coastal peoples now live in the Costa.

A Colorado man shows the traditional hair style. After cutting their hair in the form of a cap, they stain it red with a decoction made from the achota berry, then grease it with vaseline to make it shine.

The Saraguro peoples of the southern Sierra are generally wealthier than the local Hispanics. In this area, mestizos sometimes change their affiliation to join the indigenous communities as a means of improving their economic status.

The Incas moved groups of people from Bolivia and elsewhere in the Inca empire to the Ecuadorian Sierra as a means of introducing Quechua, along with the Inca religion and ways of life. The Saraguro people were moved to the southern Sierra for this purpose, and the Salasaca were moved to the central Sierra.

SIERRA Between 1.5 and two million indigenous people live in the Sierra and speak a dialect of the Quechua ("KAY-chwa") language introduced by the Incas and called Quichua ("KEE-chwa"). Most of the Sierra indigenous peoples lead an agricultural existence, farming on a small scale and supplementing their income through wage labor.

Many Sierra indígenas treat Hispanics and mestizos with deference. The Otavalo of the northern Sierra, the Salasaca of the central Sierra, and the Saraguro of the southern Sierra are more economically successful and less subservient in their mannerisms, treating Hispanics and mestizos with a certain degree of aloofness. The Salasacas were among the indigenous Serranos who most strenuously resisted the Spaniards' invasion.

The Otavalo have become internationally known for the quality of their weaving; many of them have become quite prosperous, traveling the world and selling their wares.

ORIENTE The indigenous groups of the Oriente remain the most independent, although increasing contact with Hispanic culture has caused a certain degree of assimilation. With the introduction of Western medicines, their populations are increasing. All of the Oriente peoples speak their own language or a dialect of one of the two major languages,

Shuara and Jungle Quichua. They subsist on a combination of slash-and-burn agriculture, domesticated livestock, and hunting and gathering. The three major populations are the Waorani, the Shuar, and the Ashuar; other indigenous groups include the Cofán, the Siona-Secoya, and the Zaparoan.

The Shuar number over 15,000 and consist of at least five major tribes throughout the Peruvian and Ecuadorian Amazon, primarily in and around the Cordillera de Cutucú. Previously called the Jívaro, the Quechua word for "enemy," they are now known by their own name, *Shuar*. They have very powerful *shamans*, who gain much of their *arutam* ("ah-ROO-tahm," or soul power) through warfare. Warfare, combined with a traditional fondness for the use of poison-arrow darts and shrunken heads, has given the Shuar a reputation for continuous internal feuds.

The ferocity of the population enabled the Shuar to resist colonization by the Spanish for centuries—unlike any other indigenous population in the Americas. When faced with a common enemy, the Shuar are able to put aside their internal hostilities and band together to protect their common interests. In recent decades, they have become organized into the Shuar Federation and have successfully petitioned the government for official recognition and protection of their historical territory.

The Ashuar (or Achuar) occupy the region on both sides of the Pastaza River. Their population numbers approximately 2,000. Like most of the Amazonian peoples, they are gradually losing their traditional culture. Both Catholic and Protestant missionaries have established extensive contact with the Ashuar in recent years, with the result that many have given up their traditional form of agriculture and turned to cattle-raising.

The Waorani, previously called Aucas, inhabit the region between the Napo and Curaray rivers in the Ecuadorian Amazon. This traditionally egalitarian people speak their own dialect of Jungle Quichua.

The Waorani traditionally distrust outsiders. They are generally timid, but aggressively defend their territory. In recent decades, however, the Waorani have had extensive contact with Protestant missionaries from North America.

45

A mestizo family in Quito.

MESTIZOS

Mestizos, people of mixed Hispanic and indigenous ancestry, tend to share the general cultural orientation of the Hispanic minority. The boundary between Hispanics and mestizos is more fluid than in the rest of the social hierarchy. Many mestizos mingle among the upper ranks of Ecuadorian society, and many more live and work in middle- and lower-class levels. Social rank depends on where the person lives, their degree of wealth, and their self-perception.

Mestizos are distinguished from indigenous peoples by their fluency in Spanish, their familiarity with city life, their occupation, their manners, and the fineness of their clothing. Middle-class mestizos are often low-ranking bureaucrats, hacienda (plantation) supervisors, small merchants, and clerks.

The distinction between indigenous and mestizo is more rigidly defined than is the difference between mestizo and Hispanic. In order to switch ethnic affiliation from indigenous to mestizo, the indígena must permanently leave his or her village, adopt European or Western-style clothing, learn Spanish well enough to mask his or her origin, and acquire a mestizo occupation. Many mestizos completely reject indigenous culture, perhaps in an attempt to distance themselves from their own ancestry and to seem more "white."

BLACKS

Approximately 500,000 descendants of African slaves live on the northern coast and coastal lowlands. They occupy a slightly higher social position than the indigenous peoples; and they show little subservience to Hispanics and mestizos. Ecuadorian blacks traditionally earn their living from subsistence agriculture, supplemented by wage labor, fishing, or working on cargo boats. Women on the coast often gather shellfish.

The black population is relatively diverse, classified by ethnic distinctions such as *mulatto* (African and Hispanic ancestry), *montuvio* (African, indigenous, and Hispanic ancestry), and *zambo* ("tsahm-boh," or African and indigenous ancestry). The coastal lowlands north of Manta, for instance, were conquered by African slaves from the coast of Guinea, who were shipwrecked during their passage from Panama to Peru in 1570. They killed or enslaved the indigenous men and married the indigenous females, creating the *zambo* population. They successfully resisted Spanish authority for a few decades, after which they still managed to retain a great deal of political and cultural independence.

Most of the black Ecuadorians have retained only minor remnants of their African heritage. In certain areas of the country, however, blacks continue to display evidence of their origins in dance, music, beliefs, and even in their use of the Spanish language. Descendants of African slaves continue to live in the Chota Valley in northern Ecuador. Due to their relative isolation, they have retained more of their African heritage than most Ecuadorian blacks.

A woman in the Chota Valley. Chota Valley blacks have retained some African traditions, such as African-style thatch roofing for their houses and colorful head-scarves worn by Chota women.

47

HISPANICS

The Hispanic minority sees itself as the standardbearer of civilization in Ecuador. The Spanish world view deeply penetrated Ecuadorian society with the still-persistent belief that, for the good of the whole society, each individual should be content with his or her rank. The majority of Hispanics value the "proper behavior," the appropriate sense of duty to family and kin, and the standards of a Christian, European-oriented culture. They place great importance on their Spanish ancestry.

The Minister of Mines. Financially successful Hispanics work as high-status professionals, government officials, prosperous merchants, or financiers. They tend to disparage manual labor and pursue their business interests more in order to preserve their family's social status than simply to achieve economic success.

CLASS

The elites of Ecuador originate from the large landholding class of the Sierra and the Costa. They share a fundamental belief in the value of land ownership and have traditionally used their profits from commerce and industry to buy more land and thus improve their prestige. Because they rank individuals according to birth, race, upbringing, wealth, and level of education, the elites believe that they are bred to a position of authority in Ecuadorian society. Elites describe themselves as *la gente buena* ("HEN-tay BWAY-nah") or *la gente decente* ("day-SEN-tay"), which means "the good" or "respectable people."

Unlike the Hispanic *hacendados* of the Sierra, the plantation owners of the Costa are more ethnically diverse and include many successful immigrants. Many foreigners immigrated to Ecuador from Europe and the rest of Latin American during the cocoa boom of the late 19th and early 20th centuries. Many Lebanese moved to Guayaquil, for instance, bringing their wealth with them and becoming influential members of coastal commerce and local politics.

Because of their orientation toward exports and international commerce, Costeños have traditionally been influenced by the international flow of ideas and values. Their values, lifestyles, and economic interests are completely different from the Sierra landowners.

The middle class is ethnically diverse, including not only mestizos but also immigrants from Southern Europe, the Middle East, and other Latin American countries. They are educated with at least a secondary school degree, and they consider themselves as part of *la gente buena.* The middle class includes businesspersons, professionals, clerical employees, midlevel bureaucrats and managers, army officers, and teachers.

The lower class is divided into workers and campesinos. The center of the campesinos' life is their access to land, which determines their family's livelihood and their status within the community.

The urban lower class has increased tremendously in recent decades due to massive migration to the cities from the countryside. They work as artisans or are self-employed as street vendors, tailors, carpenters, or painters, and work long hours for very low earnings.

It is said that the Saraguro men wear their black ponchos in continuous mourning for the last Inca, who was killed by the Spanish conquerors.

DRESS

The standard of dress in Ecuador is a Western style for Hispanics and mestizos, and for most blacks. A person's appearance is considered important: some working-class people dress up in a suit simply to ride the bus to work, while carrying in a briefcase their working clothes to change into when they arrive at their job.

Women in the cities wear skirts or nice slacks, dress their hair carefully, and wear facial make-up. Most campesino women wear traditional calf-length full skirts, although many are starting to wear slacks. Men generally wear slacks and button-up shirts, with a tie if possible; but for casual wear they might wear blue jeans. Businessmen in the Sierra wear dark, three-piece suits. Crowds of schoolchildren make a striking impression as they walk down the sidewalks in their three-piece uniforms.

Costeños dress more informally. Men and boys often wear shorts, thonged sandals, and tee-shirts, and women and girls wear slacks or short, loose cotton dresses. Indigenous and mestizo peasants in the southern Sierra commonly wear the misnamed Panama hat, a traditional product of Ecuador.

50

For indigenous Ecuadorians, dress both defines their ethnic identity and reinforces their exclusion from mainstream society. Clothing has become more Westernized since the 1970s, however, as increasing numbers of indigenous people who rely on wage labor for their living have begun to wear Western clothing, while choosing to stay in their indigenous community.

Serrano men traditionally wear ponchos, the color of which usually indicates their community. For instance, Otavalo men might wear a red or blue poncho, depending on where they live. The rest of their outfit generally indicates that they are an Otavalo; they wear their hair in a single long braid down their back and wear ankle-cropped white slacks and sandals. Highland men also wear a variety of broad-brimmed hat styles, depending on their group affiliation.

Serrano women usually wear embroidered blouses, woolen wrapped skirts, sandals, some type of shawl, and a locally common hat or other headgear. Otavalo women wear gold-colored glass-blown beads, the size and quantity of which indicate how wealthy they are. Many wear red cords or jewelry around their wrists or necks to ward off envy and witchcraft. They show their marital status by the color and fold of their headdress.

Indígenas of the Oriente traditionally wear little or no clothing but decorate their bodies and cut and decorate their hair in distinctive ways. They might wear symbolic feathers or bones to display their prestige and authority. In recent years, however, many of the indigenous Amazonians have begun to wear more Western clothing.

An Otavalo couple in traditional dress.

LIFESTYLE

ECUADORIANS GREATLY PRIZE their individuality. Unlike North Americans, however, they do not conceive of individuality as being "just as good as the next person," or equal to others in terms of rights and opportunities. Such concepts appear absurd to Ecuadorians, who believe in a natural social order where each individual is ranked according to such characteristics as birth, race, upbringing, wealth, and level of education. To Ecuadorians, individuality signifies that each person is absolutely special and unique, but that their rights and opportunities depend on who they are.

Each person wants to distinguish himself as an *hidalgo* ("ee-DAHL-go"), which means "son of somebody." This motivation shows why birth, race, and upbringing are so important to *la gente buena*. In practical terms, they exercise their individuality by circumventing laws that they feel are unimportant. If penalized for transgressions, the *hidalgo* exercises another important virtue, power, by calling on friends in high places to make the charges disappear.

Ecuadorians place great emphasis on the family, which they define as the immediate and extended kin, including godparents. Relationships with family and friends are of the utmost importance. They serve social, economic, and even political functions that may further the aspirations of an individual and ensure his or her security. These bonds of relationship are tightened by mutual obligations and favors.

Next to their kin, Ecuadorians prize their community. The intense rivalry between Quito and Guayaquil exemplifies the extent to which Ecuadorians exalt their locale in opposition to other towns and regions.

Opposite: **A rural scene in Cañar Province.**

Above: **Shoeshine boys watching a shooting gallery. No matter how small or large the boundaries of their social circle, Ecuadorians value and celebrate their personal relationships.**

53

Houses in the Sierra are usually constructed of brick, stone, or concrete, which is almost inevitably painted white. The effect is quite picturesque, with the rows of white houses and red tile roofs.

URBAN LIVING

Houses in the cities are generally close to one another. Middle- and upper-class people often barricade themselves behind secure, solid metal or wrought-iron gates and tall stone walls topped with shards of glass and other sharp objects.

Houses in the Costa are usually made of wood and often stand on stilts in order to withstand heavy flooding. Because of the pervasive use of wood as a building material in Guayaquil, many historical buildings, especially churches, have been lost to fire over the centuries.

Although middle- and upper-class Ecuadorians value their relationships with family and friends, they generally do not socialize with their neighbors. Their houses are usually two or three stories high, surrounded by tall fences that enclose a back courtyard or garden. Older, colonial-style houses display a rectangular form of architecture, arranged around an open-air courtyard in the center of the structure, with second-floor verandas or balconies overlooking the central area.

The majority of these houses include a servant's quarters adjacent to the laundry and kitchen areas. From this location, the servant can reach work areas without walking through the main rooms of the house.

The bottom floor of the house, aside from the kitchen and the servant's quarters, generally is used only for entertaining company. The family usually eats their meals in the kitchen and leaves the dining room for formal occasions. Likewise, the *sala*, or main room of the house, is unoccupied most of the time. The family spends much of their leisure time at home in their bedrooms or their mother's bedroom, where the television is located. The mother, or *señora*, even entertains friends in her bedroom.

In contrast, the urban poor often move into dilapidated and abandoned houses. They generally lack sewage facilities, electricity, and running water. They might also build more temporary shacks from scrap materials, adobe, reed, or cane.

MASS MIGRATIONS Once a primarily rural country with its major population base in the Sierra, Ecuador has experienced a radical population shift in the last 40 to 50 years. First, large numbers of landless and land-poor campesinos from the Sierra began flocking to the Costa during the period 1950-1974, looking for work in export agriculture. Also beginning in 1950, large numbers of Serranos migrated to the Oriente. Between 1950 and 1982, the population of the Oriente increased by five times.

At the same time, thousands more migrated to the cities. Guayaquil attracted campesinos looking for work in export agriculture during the banana boom. Quito later drew migrants looking for work during the oil boom. Land reform efforts initiated the process to some degree as the supply of wage laborers increased, making it more difficult to find agricultural work in the Sierra. The rapidly increasing migration brought an explosion of slums in the areas surrounding the cities.

Ecuador is dotted with small communities, ranging in size from one-street settlements to larger towns with a traditional town plaza surrounded by the Catholic church, the municipal government buildings, and small shops. Houses spread out from the main square. As in the large cities, they are closely set together. The adobe or concrete houses are built around small courtyards, with windows facing the patio.

A family outside their home near Quito.

RURAL LIFE

Campesino houses are generally made from materials such as bamboo, adobe, rammed earth, wattle and daub, or wood. In the Sierra, people build their houses as solidly as possible to withstand the cold; adobe brick houses are a common sight, topped with thatch roofs. In recent years, many campesinos have begun to roof their houses with metal sheeting, but they are finding that these foreign materials are not as well suited to their environment as the traditional thatch roofing. In the Costa, campesinos and wage laborers construct their houses of wood or bamboo and mount them on stilts to withstand flooding. Rural houses throughout Ecuador are often located in remote areas, such as the high páramo, the base of a volcano, or in the thick, swampy lowlands or jungle rainforest.

Country houses for the wealthy display graceful verandas, balconies, and frescos, all painted white, with the classic red tile roofing. The buildings often surround a central courtyard, which may include a small, decorative fish pond or beautiful flower banks. Extensive gardens generally surround the exterior of the structure, often decorated with strutting peacocks or parrots. A large brick wall and heavy gate protect the estate from passersby.

HEALTH

All employers are compelled to provide benefits for their employees that cover sickness, industrial accidents, disability, maternity, old age, widowhood, and orphanhood. Health care and facilities consist of an average of one hospital bed for 610 persons, and 11,033 physicians worked throughout the country.

Life expectancy for men in 1992 was 67 years, and for women 72 years. Infant mortality rates in 1991 averaged 60 deaths per 1,000 live births, which was down from an average of 70–76 per 1,000 births in the early 1980s. This rate varies radically according to region and socioeconomic status, ranging from five to 108 infant deaths per 1,000 births in urban areas, and 90 to 200 in rural areas.

Many of the old haciendas in the Sierra have been sold and are now used as resorts. In addition to the enormous size of the main building and its surrounding yard, several other buildings usually occupy the estate, such as stables and barns.

The Waorani in the Oriente build their well-ventilated houses from palm fronds and waterproof broad leaves, which they lash to frames made from stripped saplings. The result is an elongated, dome-shaped structure that can house more than 10 people in its single room. Since Waorani communities are usually very small, only a few houses are needed.

The Shuar construct their large, oval-shaped wooden houses as defensive strongholds against attacks by their enemies. They build the walls, without windows, from wooden posts that are stuck vertically into the ground about an inch apart, thus permitting light and air to enter the large room inside. They thatch the roof with closely woven palm leaves. The houses are constructed on a rise, which allows them to observe the surrounding area for intruders, as well as offering better drainage. Each family lives in isolation from its neighbors and extended family. The houses range from about 25 to 36 feet (7–11 m) in width and from 40 to 60 feet (12–18 m) in length.

In the Sierra, campesinos make long treks several times a week up and down the steep grades of the mountainsides, bent over nearly parallel to the ground as they tote agricultural goods, their babies, small livestock, or even old grandparents on their backs. Fortunate are those with burros or llamas to share their burdens!

57

The social life of men centers around the coffeehouses and the streets.

GENDER ROLES

Ecuadorian Hispanic men publicly try to conform to the image of the caudillo, whether on a personal level in their daily lives or on a political level in public life. The virtues of the caudillo have been described as "dignity, leisure, grandeur, generosity, and manliness." They strive to stand out in a crowd, whether among friends or in political circles.

In the Sierra, the regular bullfights exemplify the manly virtues of courage, individual heroism, and the raw machismo of drawing blood and risking imminent death. Throughout Ecuadorian Hispanic culture, men pride themselves on their sexual prowess, which they prove to themselves and other men through practiced flirtation with and seduction of women.

Hispanic men of all classes hiss at women on the streets, and extramarital affairs are almost expected of nonindigenous men but are a disgrace for women, if disclosed. This is not to say that women do not participate in extramarital affairs, but rather that they must be much more discreet, and the penalties for exposure are much heavier.

Within the family, the *señor* is the unquestioned head of the household.

He serves as the model of manhood for his sons and as the ideal for his daughters. Although fathers tend to treat their children with great affection, they play little part in the day-to-day running of the household. Men use their leisure time to play their public role, spending time in clubs, coffeehouses, and bars—or in the streets, depending on their social class.

If a man's identity is based on his public persona, the Ecuadorian woman's identity is based on her family and her home. Although many women work outside the home, they assume almost complete responsibility for the day-to-day working of the home. The *señora*, for instance, usually helps the maid with light housekeeping. Women are perceived as the weaker sex and are expected to play traditional feminine roles. They are expected to be virtuous, to bear children, and to serve and obey their husbands. This does not signify, however, that Ecuadorian women are generally downtrodden or weak.

As with the other aspects of the social hierarchy, Ecuadorian women in general maintain their traditional role within the social order. Indeed, they use their position to their own advantage. They are practiced in the use of feminine arts to achieve their goals, whether in the home or in professional life. They both laugh at and encourage the macho pretensions of men. They joke that men are "useless" and "big babies." Many women treat their husbands almost as one of the children, even to the point of affectionately addressing them as *mi hijo*, or "my son."

Doing the wash in Quito.

WOMEN AND CHANGE

Ecuadorian women have not made a big push to change the gender roles in their society. Most Ecuadorian women express little desire to achieve the sort of "independence" for which North American women strive. Most women recognize the role they play within the patriarchal society and do not necessarily see themselves as victims of male domination. On the contrary, they perceive many benefits, both socially and economically. Ecuadorian women perceive themselves as much more enticing and attractive to men under the status quo. As long as they fulfill their responsibilities and raise their children appropriately, they generally enjoy considerable autonomy.

Ecuadorian women view marriage positively, as part of the natural order. A single person is referred to as being "one-legged." This is especially true in the indígena communities, which believe that male and female create a whole in all parts of the universe.

The consciousness of the differences between the sexes does not inspire most Ecuadorian women to work for change in the way women are treated. Feminist consciousness among indígena women is expressed as empowering themselves—toward the end of improving conditions for the indigenous peoples as a whole. They do not see their struggle as being in opposition to men, but rather for greater freedom to work with their men.

The indígena perception of feminism derives partly from the indigenous family structure, in which women are required to take an active role. Although indigenous women still carry the responsibility for planting seeds because of the perceived spiritual strength of their fertility, there is no major gender division of labor. Men generally do the weaving, for instance, but women often weave also. Moreover, the indigenous communities in the Sierra obey strict moral guidelines that demand marital fidelity from both the husband and the wife, resulting in less subjugation of women relative to men.

Women have achieved certain constitutional gains in recent years. Although they received the rights of citizenship and voting as early as 1929, the 1967 constitution made it obligatory for them to vote. The 1979 constitution prohibits discrimination based on race, sex, religion, language, or social status. In 1987, the laws were changed to give women equal rights with their husbands in the areas of divorce, property distribution, and inheritance. Nonetheless, women still occupy only a low percentage of seats in public office.

MARRIAGE

The marriage ceremony is taken very seriously in Ecuador, especially among Hispanic and indigenous Serranos. Indígenas celebrate marriage with official religious and civil ceremonies that commit both partners to a relationship of marital fidelity. Hispanics also celebrate marriage with official religious and civil ceremonies; but marital fidelity is generally required only of the wife.

In Esmeraldas, courtship is generally brief, and premarital cohabitation is common. Men often have several serial marriages in their lifetime. Esmeraldeños have begun to unite in religious ceremonies only within the last few decades, and the men are generally unwilling to have a religious ceremony because of the commitment it implies.

Although Waorani men traditionally obtained spouses through spearing raids, it is more common today to seek spouses through peaceful interaction with other Waorani groups, who may live 60 miles (96 km) away or more through dense jungle. Waorani also increasingly intermarry with Quichua-speaking people of the lowland Oriente.

An Otavalo wedding. The marriage ceremony is celebrated with feasting, drinking, and dancing. Typical wedding food includes *humitas* ("oo-MEE-tas"), or sweet corn tamales.

FAMILY

Indigenous and nonindigenous Ecuadorians alike place great value on the family, which consists of the immediate family unit as well as extended family and others, such as godparents. A single household usually consists of the mother, father, and their unmarried children, as well as one or more members of the extended family. Newly married couples often live with one of the sets of parents for a short period, and the youngest son and his wife often continue to live at home to take care of his parents in their later years.

The wider net of kinship serves as a source of support and assistance. Upper-class families increase their power and prestige through the cultivation of far-reaching kinship ties. Lower-class families try to cultivate and strengthen those kinship ties that will be most beneficial and least costly to them. At all levels, ties are maintained through mutual gift-giving, exchanging of favors, and participation at family and community fiestas.

Members of all ethnic groups seek kinship ties outside the network of

SHUAR FAMILY STRUCTURE

The Shuar family structure is unique in Ecuadorian society, primarily because it is polygynous, and secondly because it does not always preserve kinship ties among the extended family. Each household is very closely knit in social and economic terms. They usually live in relative isolation from other people in the tribe, with at least a half-mile between dwellings.

The typical household consists of approximately 10 people, including one husband, at least two wives, and about seven children; or one husband, one wife, and three children. Other relatives, such as a widowed mother or unmarried brother, may also live in the house. Usually when one of the daughters marries, her husband also moves into the house until their first child is born, unless he is already married and must return home with his second wife.

The man is the head of the household and appears as a rather authoritarian figure within the family. He is responsible for providing for and protecting them by hunting and fishing, clearing the forest for gardens, and bringing in firewood. The woman, or women, take care of agricultural tasks, cook the food, make manioc beer and pottery, and take care of the children and livestock.

their extended families, primarily through the godparent system. Godparents, or *compadres* ("kohm-PAHD-rays"), are highly honored. Although an individual might argue or express disagreement with another family member, it would be unthinkable to treat a compadre in such a way.

BIRTH

The birth of a child is greeted with joyous celebration and ritual ceremony. In a Catholic family, within a few days of birth the child is baptized. At this time, he or she acquires a first set of compadres, who pledge to bear the responsibility of providing the child with a Christian education and upbringing. Also through this ritual, the parents and the compadres establish a lifelong relationship that persists even if the child dies.

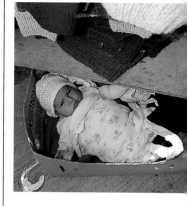

An Otavalo baby rests in a box while the parents sell their crafts in the market.

The child also receives a personal patron saint, whose fiesta day the child will celebrate throughout life, often to a greater degree than the child's own birthday. The baptism is celebrated with feasting, drinking, and dancing among the rest of the family.

Among the Shuar, a baby is given a mild hallucinogenic drug within a few days after birth. This is meant to help the baby see a vision that might give him or her supernatural powers and help in survival.

Hallucinogenic mushrooms for sale in the market. The Shuar frequently use hallucinogenic mushrooms in initiation rites.

RITES OF PASSAGE

The first religious ceremony in which Catholic Hispanics and indigenous children consciously participate is that of first communion. Children around seven years old make their first confession to the priest to cleanse them in preparation for receiving their first communion. The girls dress in white dresses and veils, symbolizing their purity.

As in much of Latin America, most Hispanic girls later participate in a ceremony and fiesta known as the *quinciñera* ("keen-see-NYA-rah"), upon reaching their fifteenth birthday. This is considered their initiation into womanhood. The celebration takes place through the church and is often quite elaborate. The girl wears a formal dress and receives communion from the priest or minister. Her father stands at her side, as he would at her wedding. The accompanying feasting and drinking costs a great deal of money, even at the simplest level. Parents often have to borrow money and become heavily indebted, especially if they have more than one daughter for whom to celebrate.

COMPADRAZGO

The institution of *compadrazgo* ("kom-pahd-RAHS-goh") among indigenous and Hispanic Christians is considered to be supremely important. Godparents, or *compadres*, are chosen not only at birth, but also at confirmation and marriage. At each occasion, the *compadres* agree to assume ritual and financial obligations to the child or newly married couple, as well as to their parents. The relationship is considered sacred.

Many indigenous and mestizo *campesinos* ask wealthy and influential whites to serve as godparents to their children. As part of the system of patronage, the poor *campesinos* expect to receive financial support and various other forms of assistance, while the godparents gain a loyal follower. It is not unusual for wealthy godparents to have several godchildren, which serves to increase their own prestige. Or parents may choose *compadres* of an equal status, in which case the level of mutual obligations and gift-giving between the parents and godparents balances out.

Young Shuar girls also undergo a ceremony of initiation, although at a much younger age. The girl is administered the same mild hallucinogenic plant she received when she was born, together with a little tobacco water. The purpose is for the girl to acquire *arutam* soul power so that when she is older she will be able to work hard and be successful producing children and raising crops and chickens and pigs. Several girls at once, usually about six, participate together in the ceremony, which is surrounded by four days of feasting and dancing at the house of the host father. For a week beforehand, the girls observe strict dietary practices, including the avoidance of any meat from mammals or birds. On the first day, the girls dance until midafternoon. Then they are given the drug and lie down at nightfall to experience visions of bountiful crops, chickens, and pigs, while the adults dance and drink until dawn. This process is repeated for the next three nights.

Shuar boys are taken to the highest waterfall at about the age of six, in order to help them see visions and begin seeking *arutam* soul power. The spray of the waterfall is believed to contain certain souls or spirits.

Shuar boys playing with a mask. At about 6 years of age, Shuar boys undergo an initiation ceremony to help them acquire soul power. They may be given a hallucinogenic drug to help facilitate the process.

65

A kindergarten class. One significant improvement for indigenous children has been the inclusion of bilingual Quichua and Spanish education in the school curriculum.

EDUCATION

Education for Ecuadorian children is compulsory for six years between the ages of six and 14. Approximately 20 percent of the schools are privately run by the Catholic Church, foreign organizations, and Protestant missionaries. Almost one-third of the urban schools are private.

Children can start preschool as young as four years old. Most children, however, begin attending school at six years for their primary education. After this, they may advance to secondary school, which consists of two cycles of three years each. The first three years expand on the primary schooling through a general education program. For the second three-year cycle, students can choose to take the university path by obtaining an education in humanities, or to prepare for technical school or teacher training.

After graduating from secondary school, those with sufficient means attend university. Twelve state universities are located in the Sierra and the Costa. The Sierra also has three private universities, and the Costa has two. There are numerous polytechnic and teacher training schools.

Although educational opportunities expanded considerably during the 1960s and 1970s, a mere 33 percent of rural children in 1991 had actually completed the required six years of primary education, in comparison to 76 percent of urban children. Illiteracy remained high, at 88 percent.

Many children, especially in the rural areas, are unable to attend school because their families need them to supplement the family income or assist in the work. In the countryside, this may mean sowing seeds, spinning wool, or tending livestock. In the urban areas, it usually means shining shoes or selling candy or crafts.

DEATH

Funerals are generally solemn affairs in Ecuador, especially if a child has died. When a child dies, he is known as an *angelito* ("ahn-hay-LEE-toh") and is believed to ascend directly to heaven. Traditional funeral foods in the Sierra include *cuy* ("kwee"), or guinea pig, which is roasted whole and served with a sauce.

In the black communities of Esmeraldas, funerals for adults are solemn and accompanied by specific songs. First, the local kin hold a wake, in which they lay out the body, either at the home or in the church, on a table covered with a white cloth. They lay flowers, leaves, and white crepe-paper wreaths on the chest of the deceased. *Cantadoras*, or singers, sing special songs, and the entire tone of the gathering is mournful. Close female relatives may weep openly. The next day, a short burial ceremony is performed by the priest in the graveyard.

Nine days of mourning follow the burial, during which the windows and doors of the house are left open— so the ghost can depart, but also so it can return. On the ninth day, the entire group of kin from far and wide gathers together to bid farewell to the deceased. The farewell ceremony is accompanied by more mournful singing, which continues until it is believed that the ties with the deceased have been severed.

RELIGION

RELIGION PLAYS AN IMPORTANT PART in the lives of many Ecuadorians. The overwhelming majority are Roman Catholic, but Protestant sects are gaining increasing influence, especially among indígenas of the Sierra and the Oriente. Ecuador nonetheless remains a Catholic culture, in the sense that Catholicism has become so deeply ingrained in the society that even people unaffiliated with the Catholic Church still share many of its values.

The Roman Catholic Church has been growing progressively uneasy at the infiltration of Protestant influence. Protestants in Ecuador have one of the highest per capita growth rates in Latin America. Real, and occasionally violent, conflict exists between the faiths. Because Ecuador officially grants freedom of religion, neither church is supported by the government.

Most of the indígenas of the Oriente and the Sierra continue to practice their traditional beliefs, which they often blend with elements of Christianity.

Monsignor Leonidas Proaño of Chimborazo Province became known as "the bishop of the indígenas" for his work on their behalf in the 1960s and 1970s. In the Oriente, a Salesian monastic mission helped the indígenas organize the Shuar Federation.

Opposite: **An Otavalo displays her strong religious feeling.**

Left: **A country shrine.**

CATHOLICISM

The Catholic Church has exerted tremendous influence over Ecuadorian society for most of the republic's history, often in partnership with the government. During the conquest and colonial period, the Spanish indoctrinated their indigenous subjects with Christianity. In many cases, the indígenas adapted the new religion to their own traditional cosmology.

Representatives of the Church took advantage of this as an intermediate step to conversion while trying to submerge the indigenous religions by superimposing Catholic symbols on indigenous religious practices. For instance, the Spanish constructed Catholic shrines over many of the existing sacred spots of the Incas in the mountains. Many of the festivals still combine symbols from traditional indigenous beliefs and Catholicism.

Recent reports of a sighting of the Virgin Mary by a young girl has inspired thousands of people to visit a remote spot in the southern highlands. They travel by car or by bus, by donkey or by foot, to receive her messages, say prayers, offer petitions, and leave mementos.

Saraguros attend a Catholic service.

A CATHOLIC LANDSCAPE

Travelers to Ecuador used to comment that Quito was a city with 100 churches and only one bathroom. The capital has modernized considerably since the oil boom, but its colonial churches continue to preside majestically over the impoverished hustle and bustle of Old Quito.

Spaniards used indigenous labor to build many of their churches, which include some of the finest architecture in the Americas. La Compañía de Jesus in Quito (shown here) is the most ornate church in Ecuador. Its stunning interior is gilded with seven tons of gold leaf, and the majestic stone exterior was carved by hand. Construction began in 1605 and took 163 years to complete.

Construction began on the Monastery of San Francisco only a few weeks after Quito was founded in 1534 and was finished 70 years later; the church is the largest colonial structure in Quito. Other large cities, such as Cuenca and Guayaquil, also have beautiful old churches and cathedrals; and every small community has at least one church facing the main plaza. The most important churches in the Costa are all restored replicas of the original, wooden colonial structures that have burned down one or more times.

The physical presence of Catholicism does not stop with architecture. Small shrines are visible throughout the countryside of the Sierra; and the most impressive public sculpture, La Virgen de las Americas, watches over Quito from her pedestal on a hill named El Panecillo.

Nearly 95 percent of Ecuadorians profess affiliation with the Catholic Church. Some people devote themselves to Catholicism and may attend mass on a daily basis. Others just participate in special ceremonies and rituals, such as baptism and the first communion. Some people dedicate their lives to the service of a particular saint or make pilgrimages to holy sites around the country.

Catholicism so strongly permeates the society, especially in the Sierra, that people often take its influence for granted. They may participate in Catholic rituals, such as godparent relationships, for reasons that are as much cultural as religious. Cultural Catholicism also emphasizes family relationships, social hierarchies, and traditional attitudes about women.

PROTESTANTISM

As in much of Latin America, Protestantism is growing by leaps and bounds. Ecuador experienced a 5.7 percent growth rate in the percentage of evangelical Protestants, during the period 1960 to 1985—the fourth highest rate of increase in Latin America. In 1990, approximately 3.2 percent of the population was affiliated with the evangelicals. The rapidly increasing Protestant influence has drawn both praise and criticism. On one hand, Protestant missionaries in rural areas have built schools, medical clinics, toilets, and other socially beneficial structures. Part of their success in attracting converts from Catholicism (in spite of active opposition from Catholic priests) is due to the fact that they have made special efforts to recognize and respect the indígenas as equals. Unlike the Catholic Church, Protestant missionaries speak to the indígenas in Quichua, through a translation of the Bible and radio broadcasts. This is a powerful medium to reach a population that had formerly been expected to receive God's message through the language of the whites, who despised them. Many Protestant converts in the Sierra have thus experienced a renewal of ethnic pride.

On the other hand, many indigenous people and anthropologists criticize the Protestant missionaries, saying that their influence still leads to acculturation because they encourage indígenas to fit a "civilized" model of "the good Indian." They have also been accused of indirectly encouraging people not to participate in communal work projects or in

A Saraguro woman at a shrine.

communal fiestas. Evangelical Protestant missionaries claim that these pursuits are a waste of time and money. Whereas Catholic peasants communally celebrate fiestas in honor of the local patron saint who is expected to mediate with God on their behalf, the Protestants emphasize an individual relationship with God. The Virgin Mary and the Catholic legion of saints thus lose their power, eliminating the need for a community fiesta in their honor. When converts to Protestantism stop attending the fiestas, other members of their community charge that they have become antisocial—a serious accusation in a culture that places great emphasis on community relationships and cooperation.

Many Ecuadorians have also accused Protestants of trying to "buy" religious influence among the poor by sponsoring social action and giving impoverished communities food and money. Protestant missions have been more obviously responsible for a great deal of acculturation, especially among the Oriente indígenas, whose children often forget their native language as they grow up in Christian boarding schools. It should be noted, however, that a similar process of acculturation has been taking place for centuries among the Sierra indígenas who attended Catholic schools that taught them to be ashamed of their ethnicity.

A religious festival.

Otavalo women in church. Many indigenous peoples have incorporated elements of native belief systems into their practice of Catholicism.

INDIGENOUS BELIEF SYSTEMS

The religious beliefs of the Sierra indígenas vary considerably from those of the Oriente. Although most indigenous Serranos are affiliated with the Catholic Church, many have also held onto aspects of their traditional beliefs, blending the two belief systems to form their own world view.

SIERRA Many Serrano indígenas retain vestiges of an ancient animistic belief system. Many indígenas ascribe qualities such as hot/cold, male/female, weak/strong, and good/evil to natural phenomena. For instance, the Quichua-speaking peoples of the Sierra traditionally call the Earth *pacha mama*, or "earth mother." This name conveys their affinity to the earth as the source of life. The fertility of the earth is strongly associated with women. Many feel that the planting will be especially fertile if sown by a pregnant woman. Serranos demonstrate their relationship to the earth by spilling out the last drops of alcohol onto the ground at fiestas and other gatherings, in a gesture of offering to *pacha mama*. The Andean mountains that surround them are seen individually as either male or female, with strong spiritual forces.

ORIENTE The spiritual beliefs of the indigenous peoples of the Oriente have been strongly influenced by Catholic and Protestant missions during recent decades. Some indigenous peoples have lost their traditional beliefs through Christian education projects, while others have grafted Christian ideas onto their traditional belief systems.

The spiritual tradition of the Shuar reflects their individualistic quest for power. They believe that all men, women, plants, animals, spiritual beings, and some inanimate objects have *kakáram* ("kah-KAH-rahm"), a vital force necessary to survive and to achieve personal goals in the face of opposition. The Shuar believe in an ever-present supernatural world, which humans can see only when in a hallucinogenic state or when dreaming. They identify this world as the "real world," with which every Shuar must become familiar in order to learn the true nature of the universe and the tools to protect himself or herself in the waking world. Any adult man or woman may become a shaman, one who is able to cross over to the supernatural world. Most of the indigenous people of the Oriente are egalitarian in their social order, and anyone with sufficient innate power can become a shaman through apprenticeship for several years.

The Shuar believe that the power of knowledge grows stronger with its distance from local sources. Indeed, a Shuar seeks to obtain knowledge from outside sources, whether from indigenous Serranos, Hispanics, or other outsiders. They count their ability to cross cultural boundaries through language and dress as an additional sign of strength.

Many indigenous Serranos describe the sun as vengeful and dangerous, striking with illness at individuals who defiantly choose not to wear their hat outdoors. The moon is also personalized with certain negative characteristics: seeds will not germinate if planted during a new moon, and fabrics will fall apart if dyed during the new moon. Rainbows are masculine and live in certain rivers; women who bathe or wash clothes in these rivers may become pregnant.

An occultist in Quito.

FOLK BELIEFS

Many campesinos combine traditional beliefs, Catholic teachings, and medieval Spanish beliefs. They believe that many spirits and supernatural forces inhabit and threaten their world. Campesinos in the Sierra fear the *duende* ("DWEN-day"), an elf-like being with large eyes and a huge hat who likes to prey on large-eyed children with abundant hair. The *huacaisiqui* ("hwa-kai-SEE-kee") are spirits of aborted or abandoned infants who steal babies' souls. Campesinos may also believe in spirits of the mountain mist, rainbows, and other natural phenomena. These or other supernatural forces may strike a person who is vulnerable.

The in-between periods of dawn and dusk and the hours of noon and midnight appear as cracks through which supernatural spirits and forces can enter or escape the human world. Noon and midnight are considered to be dangerous times to be abroad because of their ambiguity: they are neither morning nor afternoon, neither night nor morning.

Within the highland indigenous communities, this world view inspires the aloof behavior that often characterizes indígenas. Since isolation and

Folk Beliefs

encounters with strangers can lead to supernatural attacks, they try to avoid strangers and remain in human company. Among the Saraguros, for instance, women regard the outside world as threatening and filled with disease, while the home serves as a refuge from illness and danger.

Blacks in Esmeraldas also have a wealth of spiritual beliefs, many transplanted from Africa. The *tunda*, for example, is a malevolent water creature and a child of the devil. She appears as a deformed woman with huge lips and a club foot. Unable to bear children herself, she steals the children of the Esmeraldeños. Parents protect their children by not letting them go out without protective dogs.

At midnight, a faceless phantom called La Mala Hora *(the evil hour) pursues men who are walking about. She appears to her victim disguised as a beautiful woman whom he knows and desires, but she keeps her face hidden. Contact with her is usually fatal.*

FOLK HEALERS

Every community has a person skilled in the art of healing. People seek out the healers, called *curanderos* ("coo-rahn-DAY-rohs"), and witches, called *brujos* ("BROO-hos"), looking for everything from love potions to a cure for a malnourished baby.

Campesinos generally do not arrive at a Western diagnosis such as malnourishment for their sick child; rather, they are more likely to identify the child as a victim of supernatural forces or the *mal* ("mahl"). When someone becomes ill, the healer or family classifies the sickness as supernatural, a medical infection, or a humoral imbalance. They seek a doctor's treatment only if they think that the illness is caused by infection. However, everyone agrees that illness can be avoided through strength and good nutrition, because the *mal* preys on weakness.

Many rural Serranos believe in the same "humoral" theory of disease that once dominated European medicine. In this theory, disease results from an imbalance of four bodily fluids, or "humors": blood, black bile, yellow bile, and phlegm. Each of these fluids is defined as "hot," "cold," "wet," or "dry." An excess of any humor upsets the body's equilibrium and causes illness.

Some medical doctors have come to recognize and respect the work of the curanderos; likewise, many curanderos recognize the powers of Western medicine. If either the medical doctor or the healer is unsuccessful in curing a patient, they may recommend that the patient seek attention from the alternative path of medicine. This cooperative relationship is increasingly common in areas with large indigenous populations, as in the Sierra and the Oriente.

LANGUAGE

SPANISH IS THE OFFICIAL LANGUAGE of Ecuador, although a significant portion of the population speak indigenous languages and a small number speak a creole language. Each language has borrowed from the others. The Quichua word for baby, *guagua* ("GWA-gwa"), is commonly used as slang in Spanish. A person might ask his friend, "*¿Cómo están los guaguas?*" or "How are your kids?"

The diversity of language reflects and reinforces the regional and racial divisions within Ecuadorian society. Although Spanish is the common language, how it is spoken differs according to region, ethnic group, and socioeconomic class. Spanish speakers look down on speakers of Quichua. Conversely, those who speak Quichua often regard Spanish speakers as "rude" and "vulgar" because they lack the sophistication and subtlety of expression the Quichua language offers.

Opposite: **Reading the newspaper.**

Left: **Social divisions are also played out in non-verbal forms of communication through attitudes of aloofness, hostility, or condescension.**

INDIGENOUS LANGUAGES

Many indigenous people throughout the Sierra and the Oriente speak Quichua. The unrelated Shuar language spreads nearly as far in the Oriente as Quichua does. Smaller language groupings in the Oriente include Cofán, Siona-Secoya, Waorani, and Zaparoan.

None of the indigenous peoples had a written language prior to the conquest, nor do any of their languages have their own indigenous alphabet. Outsiders, primarily missionaries, have phonetically transcribed their languages into either English or Spanish. Because of the various alphabets that have been devised for the languages, many words can be spelled different ways. The name by which the former "Aucas" identify themselves, for instance, can be spelled *Waorani* (English) or *Huarani* (Spanish). Also, the Quichua word for baby, *guagua*, can also be spelled *wawa* or *huahua*.

Indigenous organizations have recently begun to protest for official recognition of their native languages but have achieved only minor success. They have succeeded in obtaining bilingual education in many schools, which will help stop the erosion of their language among the younger generations. Nonetheless, although the Minister of Education has been willing to permit bilingual education in the schools, he has prohibited the actual substitution of any indigenous language for Spanish-language instruction, thus indicating the government's unwillingness to recognize a second official language.

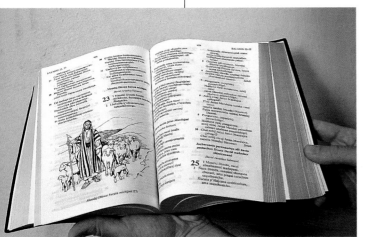

The Bible has been translated into Quichua.

Indígenas engaged in a conversation.

The Incas spread Quechua as the common language throughout their empire, though it also spread beyond the borders of their empire without the force of conquest. Today, Quechua is spoken by more than eight million people from Colombia to Argentina, making it the most commonly spoken indigenous language in the Americas.

Approximately 35,000 indígenas of the Oriente speak Quichua. The language spread throughout the Ecuadorian Amazon during the same period that it spread through the Sierra. The jungle Quichua cultures share other characteristics in addition to their language, such as agricultural sophistication, hunting and fishing techniques, and the cosmological perception of their environment.

The languages of the Oriente were formerly lumped together and called Jivaroan. For much of Ecuador's history, this was the name given to all the Oriente tribes and their languages.

The second language family in the Oriente, next to Quichua, is Shuar. The Shuar share their language as well as cultural characteristics with several Amazonian peoples of Peru.

SPANISH

When the Spanish came, they introduced Spanish as the common language. During the colonial period, various creole languages also developed, which are still spoken today in some parts of Ecuador. *Media lengua* ("MAY-dee-ah LAYN-gwa"), for example, uses Spanish vocabulary with Quichua grammar. Some blacks in the Costa speak a creole Spanish.

Regional differences in spoken Spanish are notable. For instance, Serranos speak a clear Castilian Spanish, while Costeños tend to swallow the last syllable of most words and eliminate most of the *s* sounds. In Guayaquil, the phrase *más o menos* ("mahs oh MAY-nohs") ends up sounding like "maomay." This speech pattern is the main Costeño characteristic that Serranos point to when calling them *monos*, or "monkeys."

Only the most isolated Ecuadorians of the high Sierra or the deep jungles of the Oriente do not speak or understand Spanish today. Many indigenous people are bilingual and use Spanish when speaking to *indígenas* of other language groups.

COMMUNICATION CUSTOMS

Ecuadorians prize gestures of courtesy, particularly in the Sierra. Even when discussing business, Ecuadorians will always spend at least a minute of conversation chatting graciously before initiating the substance of the conversation. They often regard people from the United States as rude and abrupt, because North Americans jump right into a conversation without engaging in the requisite preliminary courtesies. Even conversations between strangers begin with the cordial greeting, *"Buenos días, ¿Cómo está?"* ("Good day, how are you?").

A television newscaster.

Another custom of courtesy among Ecuadorians, especially in the Sierra, is to politely pretend agreement regardless of circumstances or true feelings. Part of the Serrano system of courtesy is making extravagant promises without the expectation of fulfilling them. Also, if asked a question about something of which they have no knowledge, they will often dissemble and say anything to hide the fact that they do not know. This well-intended behavior provides the basis for the contempt that Costeños often express toward the Serranos, whom they accuse of being false and superficial.

Ecuadorians also use the word *mañana*, which literally means "tomorrow," to connote almost everything *but* tomorrow. If a person says that they will do something *mañana*, they may mean that they will do it later, that they do not want to do it, that they will do it eventually, or that they will never do it.

83

Local women conversing
in front of La Compania
Church in Quito.

NONVERBAL COMMUNICATION

Like most Latin Americans, Hispanic and mestizo Ecuadorians greet each other and say goodbye with a single kiss on the cheek. Women friends greet each other with a kiss, as do men and women acquaintances, except when conducting business. Men do not kiss other men, however; rather, they exchange handshakes with their male acquaintances and hugs with close friends. Between men and women, and among women, a single meeting is enough of a basis to salute each other with a kiss. This is a courtesy performed only between acquaintances of the same social class, however.

Relations with indígenas tend to be more formal. Most indigenous

Serranos address Hispanics and mestizos with humility and treat them with great deference. Hispanics and mestizos, in turn, patronizingly treat them as children who need to be guided. They address the indígenas using the familiar pronouns and verb forms. The notable exceptions to this sort of patron-client relationship are among the Salasaca and the Saraguro peoples, who pride themselves on their attitude of bravado toward outsiders.

A form of sexism that occurs daily in communication between men and women is the macho hissing at women on the street. Men of all classes, though not of all ethnic groups, habitually hiss at women passersby, making a sound similar to *ts-ts-tssss* by pressing their tongue to the back of their teeth. Although she sometimes shows discreet irritation, the woman never openly responds.

ECUADORIAN NAMES AND TITLES

Hispanics and most mestizos follow the Spanish custom of having a double surname, taking the patrimonial surname from both parents to form their own surname. For instance, a young woman by the name Marlena Pasos Durán has two surnames: Pasos from her father's family, and Durán from her mother's family. Formally, she is known as Señorita Pasos. When she marries a man named Humberto Rodríguez Bucaram, she will take his surname and add it to hers: Marlena Pasos de Rodríguez. Formally, she will then become known as Señora de Rodríguez.

Various kinds of titles are used in Ecuador, where the attitude seems to be "the more illustrious the better." The usual titles of respect include señor, señora, and señorita. Señora is usually used for married or older women, while señorita is used for younger or unmarried women.

Ecuador passed legislation several years ago prohibiting people from using foreign names for their children. The law was inspired by the large numbers of people who named their children with names that they saw in newspapers or heard on the radio. One Ecuadorian woman told a story of meeting a Quichua couple whose baby was named Washco — short for Washington.

ARTS

ECUADOR HAS A WELL-DEVELOPED artistic tradition that dates back at least 5,000 years to the Valdivia culture. Pre-Columbian craftsmanship is generally thought of as archeology instead of art, primarily because the names of its artists are unknown and their work therefore is attributed to the culture in which they lived. Nonetheless, several of the indigenous cultures of Ecuador left evidence of highly developed artistic cultures. The Valdivia culture, from 4800 B.C. to 1200 B.C., produced painted ceramics of extraordinary beauty for purely artistic expression as well as for practical use, including ceramic figurines representing people, gods, and shaman-like figures. The images from these cultures have influenced several modern Ecuadorian painters.

VISUAL ARTS

Ecuador boasts a long history of well-developed painting styles. The two most notable artistic trends include the colonial Quito School and the 20th-century school of *indigenismo* ("in-dee-hain-EES-mo"). The Quito School developed during the colonial period as a style based on religious subject matters, such as the Virgin Mary, other saints, and Christ, who were often portrayed in graphic agony. Indigenismo is a contemporary movement that uses indigenous subject matter. It has influenced both the visual and literary arts.

Opposite: **Otavalo woven blankets for sale in the market. International appreciation of indigenous products has created a strong demand for traditional designs.**

Above: **A woodcarver working in balsa wood.**

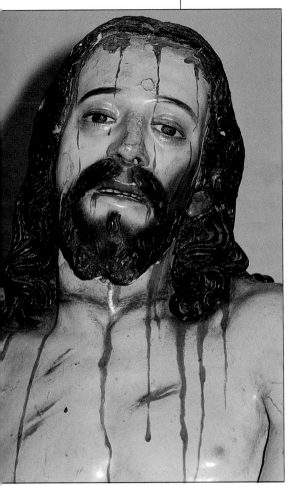

A statue of Christ in the style of the Quito School.

THE QUITO SCHOOL The Spaniards brought to the Americas their European conceptions of art, which often revolved around Catholic religious themes. Beginning in the 16th century, they started training local indigenous artists to produce sculpture, painting, and gold work with religious themes. This combination of Spanish religious concepts executed by indigenous artists developed into the Quito School of Art, which lasted through the 17th and 18th centuries.

The Quito School also influenced architecture, characterized by an almost overwhelming degree of ornamentation in many of Quito's colonial churches. Many churches are crowded with paintings and sculptures from the Quito School. A particularly common subject in both media is an anguished Christ on the cross, his wounds appearing to ooze realistic blood. The paintings have an imposing presence with their enormous size and dark and solemn tone.

INDIGENISMO The 20th century brought the rise of indigenismo, which is characterized more by its subject matter than by a common artistic style. The unifying theme consists of an awareness and denunciation of the oppression of Ecuador's indigenous peoples. Painting styles range from realist to impressionist, cubist, and surrealist. The most famous indigenista painters include Eduardo Kingman, Camilo Egas, and Oswaldo Guayasamín.

Eduardo Kingman has been described as the

prototypical indigenista. His work since the 1930s has consisted of murals, oil paintings, and book illustrations that experiment with color and subjects of oppression. Oil paintings display characteristic semi-abstract human images with heavy facial features and huge, distorted hands.

The early works of Camilo Egas are surrealist in style. In the 1950s, he switched to realism and produced paintings that conveyed a sense more of dignity than of misery. From the late 1950s until his death in 1961, Egas switched to abstract impressionism.

Oswaldo Guayasamín is practically identified with modern art in Ecuador. His father was an indígena whose heritage greatly influenced Guayasamín's work. Guayasamín is most commonly identified with his cubist paintings of tortured and oppressed indigenous peoples. The tone of suffering in these representations of indígenas is influenced by the religious artwork of the Quito School. He often uses enormous canvases, almost overwhelming the viewer with life-sized, graphic images of misery.

A mural in Guayaquil.

THE NEW GENERATION Younger painters have moved away from indigenismo to the portrayal of more personalized themes. Ramiro Jácome of Quito started out in the 1970s painting in a neofigurative style. In the early 1980s he created a series of abstract oil paintings characterized by rich, deep colors. He later returned to figurative works that portray aspects of Ecuadorian daily life. Other recent artists of note include Jaime Romero and Washington Iza.

LITERARY ARTS

Ecuador has produced many fine writers, most significantly during the 20th century. Although novels, poetry, and essays are common, the most important literary form is the short story. Very few women writers are included in the lists of Ecuador's finest, although a few have achieved notice in recent decades. One such exception is Alicia Yanez Cossio. In several novels since the 1970s, she has explored the position of women in Ecuadorian society, often with great use of satire.

One of the most notable writers of the 19th century was Juan Montalvo (1832-1889), a prolific essayist who wrote about contemporary politics and was a strong critic of dictators such as Gabriel García Moreno. His best-known work is the 1882 compilation of essays, *Siete Tratados* (Seven Treatises), which includes a comparison between the revolutionary heros Simón Bolívar and George Washington.

The most significant writer of the 20th century was Jorge Icaza (1906-1979), who authored the first indigenista novel in Latin America. *Huasipungo* (1934) brutally depicts the oppression of indigenous campesinos by the hacienda owners, who first seize their communal lands and then massacre those who protest. The novel wrenchingly portrays how trapped the *indígenas* are in their suffering by the rest of society, especially by the landowners, the Church, and the military. In 1974, the novel was translated into English as *The Villagers*. Icaza was also known as a playwright, actor, and writer of short stories.

Many significant authors have come from the Costa, including the "Guayaquil Group," whose writing explored life among the *montuvios* (those of mixed black, indígena, and Hispanic ancestry). José Antonio Campos (also known as Jack the Ripper) established himself as the precursor to the Ecuadorian short story form.

DANCE

Although the mainstream mestizo culture dances primarily as a form of entertainment and leisure activity, they commemorate certain traditional Ecuadorian dances during festivals. During Corpus Cristi, for instance, many people in the areas surrounding Quito have traditionally danced the *yumbo* ("YOOM-boh"), where they dress in plumed costumes and stop traffic with mock ambushes. Some people still perform the folkloric Spanish dance called the *cueca* ("KWAY-kah"), in which couples dance together holding handkerchiefs, although it is primarily danced at festivals.

At weddings and parties, people dance to *cumbias* ("KOOM-byas") and *sanjuanitos* ("sahn-hwa-NEE-tohs"), whether played by traditional musicians or by bands with amplified instruments. Indígenas have a variety of dances to celebrate courtship and other rituals. Many indigenous dances involve rings of couples with a play of hats or handkerchiefs.

MUSIC

Ecuadorians generally love music—especially dance music, such as the Caribbean *salsa* or *merengue* ("may-RAIN-gay") and the Colombian *cumbia*. The cumbia is very popular on the coast, and is often identified as Costeño music. Brass instruments, such as trumpets, tubas, trombones, clarinets, cymbals, and French horns, are often played for small-town fiestas.

Ecuador established a national conservatory of music in 1870. Many classical artists, such as Domenico Brescia (*Ecuadoran Symphony*) and Segundo Luis Moreno (*Three Ecuadorian Suites*), have included indigenous melodies in their compositions. Luis Humberto Salgado composed a symphonic suite entitled *Atahualpa* that utilizes indigenous elements.

SHUAR MUSIC Shuar music is based on a three-note scale. The Shuar sing three types of songs, or *nampesmas*: love songs, gardening songs, and social or public songs. They used to sing a fourth type, war songs, until the missionaries came. Women sing most often and teach *nampesmas* to their daughters, but men can sing also. Women are not allowed to play instruments, however. The Shuar men play a flute, violin, or musical bow.

Nampesmas do not include music played for ceremonial purposes, such as the shaman's curing ceremonies. Ritual music uses different instruments, such as the large slit drum, the two-headed drum, and the seed or shell rattle belts.

The Andean harp is a more rustic version of the European harp.

Andean musicians playing traditional panpipes and stringed instruments introduced by the Spanish.

ANDEAN MUSIC Traditional Andean music is based on a five-note scale and uses three basic types of instruments: wind, percussion, and rattles and bells. The Spanish introduced string instruments, which were quickly adopted. The combination of these instruments with the pentatonic scale produces a hauntingly breathy sound.

Wind instruments include flutes, panpipes, and conch shells. The *quena* ("KAY-nah") is a notched bamboo flute that was once made from the leg bones of a condor. Percussion instruments include drums called *bombos*. The musicians also use bells, or *campañas* ("cahm-PAH-nyahs"), and various rattles, including gourd rattles, known as *maracas*. The panpipe, or *rondador* ("rohn-dah-DOHR"), is fashioned of varying lengths and diameters of either cane or bamboo pipes tied together in a long row.

The Spanish introduced string instruments to Ecuador, such as the guitar, violin, and mandolin. Ecuadorian musicians adopted the *charanga* ("cha-RAHN-gah") and the Andean harp. The small *charanga* originated in Bolivia and is made traditionally from the shell of an armadillo. More recently, Andean musicians have incorporated the accordion and the harmonica into their instrumentation.

Bands play primarily at fiestas and in folk music clubs, called peñas. *Men usually play the instruments and sing, while women only sing. The most common type of music is the* sanjuanito, *Ecuador's national dance music. Lyrics are usually in Quichua.*

93

Ecuadorian artisans have developed their crafts over centuries, and many individual towns around the country are particularly noted for the quality of a specific craft. Otavalo, for instance, has for centuries been a center for woven textiles. San Antonio de Ibarra, in the northern Sierra, is a center of fine woodwork. Cotacachi is known for its leatherwork. The small town of Calderón produces human and animal figures made of painted bread dough.

PANAMA HATS

The so-called "Panama hat," or *sombrero de paja* ("sohm-BRAY-roh day PAH-ha"), is an indigenous product of Ecuador. They became known as Panama hats because they came through a center in Panama on their way to the United States.

Panama hats are woven from thin *toquilla* ("toh-KEE-ya") straw, which grows on bushes in the coastal lowlands. *Pajeros* ("pah-HAY-rohs"), or straw cutters, harvest the *toquilla* straw, then transport it to warehouses in Guayaquil. From there, it is shipped to the straw markets in Cuenca and other weaving centers. Every week, tens of thousands of campesinos come from the countryside around Cuenca and parts of the Costa to the nearest weaving center. They carefully choose the lengths of straw for a single hat, the quality of which will determine their weekly income. Most weavers are women who as children learned the craft from their mothers as a means of supplementing the family income.

Although most of the weavers work in the southern Sierra, the finest hats are made in Montecristi, near the coast. Panamas come in all qualities, from coarsely woven to "superfine." The weavers of Montecristi labor over their superfine hats so painstakingly that the finished product can hold water; the first six inches can take as long as 15 days, while the rest of the crown may take three weeks to complete. Other weavers finish six or more coarsely woven hats per week. Most sell their hats for about 65 cents.

OTAVALO WEAVERS

The indígenas of the Otavalo area, north of Quito, have distinguished themselves by their weaving for centuries. The traditional weaving tool was a backstrap loom, which some people still use. The Spanish introduced the treadle loom, the spinning wheel, handcarders, wool, and silk, and some people now use electric looms and synthetic fibers. In 1917, local weavers began to produce fine fabrics to compete with British imports, and the Otavalo weavers entered the cash economy.

The weavers obtain their wool locally from sheep and llamas, and occasionally from alpacas in Peru. Many Otavalo front doors open into a family workshop within the home. Men traditionally do the weaving, although many women weave also.

The Otavalos are farmers as well as artisans because they cannot participate fully in the indigenous community without owning land. Generations of land division among their children has led to extreme fragmentation of family holdings, so weaving has become essential to supplement the family income.

An Otavalo weaver. Weaving has become a successful cottage industry for Otavalos.

LEISURE

ECUADORIAN CULTURE HOLDS leisure as an important value. *La gente buena* prize their enjoyment of leisure quite highly, often over personal economic success. Ecuadorians traditionally work to provide for their needs and little more.

Such an ethos was born from a society that lived off the work of others, but it is an ideal that all Ecuadorians aspire to. For the majority of campesinos and urban poor, work is neverending, and the only break in the monotony of their struggle to survive is at fiesta time. For mainstream Ecuadorians, however, leisure is a way of life that is interrupted by work.

Many businesses close for a few hours during the middle of the day, while people go home and eat the midday meal with their families. After lunch they enjoy a short rest, or *siesta*, then return to work until six or seven in the evening. They also close Saturday afternoons and Sundays.

The Hispanic ethos of leisure, and the socioeconomic system that has for so long supported it, is revealed in an Ecuadorian saying, "The clever one lives off the foolish and the foolish lives off his labor."

Opposite: **Relaxing on a park bench in Guayaquil.**

Left: **The elites relax at their country clubs, where they can enjoy golf, heated swimming pools, saunas, and horseback riding. For an extended holiday, they might escape to their hacienda, if the family still owns it.**

Taking a break from working in the gold mine. Sports are also a popular weekend activity.

ORDINARY WEEKENDS

For most Ecuadorians, vacations center around holidays, of which there are plenty. During the normal course of the week, however, most people find time to relax by socializing with family and friends.

On Sundays, people gather after church in the town plaza and visit. The men may attend a cockfight. In Quito and Ibarra, playing glove ball is extremely popular on Sunday afternoons. Almost every weekend there are soccer matches to attend at the local stadium or soccer field. In the Sierra, bullfights are also quite popular. Young women compete in beauty contests, which are held frequently at all levels of society.

If they don't go out in the evening, the family may stay at home and watch television or, in more isolated areas, listen to the radio. In middle and upper class homes, the family congregates in the parents' bedroom, where the television is kept. In small towns and rural areas, neighbors may gather at a friend's house to listen to the radio or watch television.

Although storytelling used to be an extremely popular form of leisure activity in places such as Esmeraldas and the Oriente, the custom is dying out due to the prevalence of television and radio.

For the urban middle and upper class, evening is the time to dress up and go out—dancing, to the theater, to hear a concert, or simply to visit friends. Young people especially like to go out in groups to discotheques or *peñas*, where they can dance to salsa or cumbia music, or to folkloric music. They might also attend the cinema, where they can watch movies from the United States, Europe, Mexico, or Argentina. Small towns tend to offer little more than the local cinema as entertainment, except during the town's fiesta day.

On the weekends, the beaches and city parks fill up with families having picnics, children horseback riding, and men and boys playing soccer, basketball, or volleyball.

BULLFIGHTING

Bullfighting is a popular tradition in Ecuador, especially in the Sierra. During the first week of December, Quito celebrates the founding of the city and hosts one of its twice-yearly bullfight competitions. During the Quito Day celebrations, Ecuadorian bullfighters, or *toreros* ("toh-RAY-rohs"), compete with international bullfighters in a series of 10 bullfights.

Bullfighting in its modern form dates back to 18th-century Spain. In its ritualized brutality, bullfighting exalts the heroic virtues of machismo:

Bullfighting at a harvest festival.

braided silk suits and spears, graceful pomp and spurting blood, camaraderie and individual heroism. The audience praises the accomplished *torero* ("toh-RAIR-oh") with wild enthusiasm and cascading flowers, but boos and heckles the torero who botches the job or fails to kill the bull quickly enough. The bulls are carefully bred and selected from reputable haciendas in Ecuador. The spectators love to see a *bravo* ("BRAH-voh") bull, one who is aggressive but dignified and stately. Indeed, the bull represents heroism and machismo as well.

After allowing the bull to circle the ring a few times, a team of *picadores* ("pee-kah-DOH-rays"), mounted on padded and blindfolded horses, approach the bull. Drawing his attention to them, they quickly mince in close and cast small, colorfully festooned spears into the bull's upper back, making the blood run down his body. This enrages the bull and the procedure is repeated until the bull is running and snorting around the ring with four to six of the bright *picos* ("PEE-kohs") in his massive shoulders.

At this point, the *matador* ("mah-tah-DOR," the torero who kills the bull), makes his entrance. He walks out into the bullring. He bows to the audience, to the judges and to the bull, then presents his scarlet cape. He waves it in front of the bull a few times, drawing the animal's rage toward him and allowing the bull to pass fiercely under the cape. The *matador* must be extremely quick and graceful in stepping aside to avoid being gored. When the relationship has been established, the matador and the bull face off. The bull charges him once more—and, if the matador is skilled or lucky enough, he plunges his sword through the animal's spine, killing him with a single thrust.

If the matador has executed the fight well, the bullring explodes with cheers, flowers, and brass band music. Depending on the skill and grace that he has shown, the matador may be awarded one or two ears —or the ultimate prize, two ears and the tail.

Small towns and local fiestas hold juegos de toros *("HWAY-gohs day TOH-rohs"), or "bull-baiting" contests more often than actual bullfights. The Salasacas of the central Sierra provide many of their exceptionally fine bulls for this purpose. The Salasaca bulls are respected for being as bravo as their breeders.*

NOMBRE

Ing. ROSERO

The owners breed and train their gamecocks especially for fighting, which they begin between one and two years of age.

COCKFIGHTING

Cockfighting is popular all over Ecuador, as evidenced by the fact that most towns have a cockfighting coliseum. Cockfighting is a sport of ancient origins, in which the owners of the gamecocks, or *gallos* ("GAH-yohs"), place their birds into a circular ring about 20 feet (7 m) in diameter and let them fight each other, sometimes to the death. Their handlers equip the cocks with metal or bone spurs, averaging about 1 $^1/_2$ inches (4 cm) in length, to increase their ability to damage the other birds in the ring.

After placing the artificial spur over the natural spur of the gamecock, the handlers "set" their birds into the ring at the same time. The male birds, becoming infuriated at the proximity of the other bird, run and jump at each other, trying to spur and wound one another in the eyes or chest. If one of the cocks refuses to fight longer, the handler puts him breast to breast with the other bird. If he still refuses, the judge rules that the *gallo* has quit, and the fight ends.

Cockfighting fans become passionate about the matches, primarily because of the heavy gambling that surrounds them. Odds on birds fluctuate constantly, and the spectators often wager great sums of money.

SPORTS

Soccer, or *fútbol* ("FOOT-bohl"), is the national game and is played at all levels in the Costa and the Sierra. A national team competes in international competition, and professional and amateur athletes play throughout the

A soccer game between Ecuador and Chile.

country, either on organized teams or informally on Sunday afternoons. Every match, especially the World Cup, creates great excitement among the spectators. Streets empty as the fans crowd the stadiums for local and national games, and people all over the country crowd around their radios and television sets. If their team wins, they pour out onto the streets and celebrate.

Another very popular game in Ibarra and Quito is glove ball, or *pelota de guante* ("pay-LOH-tah day HWAN-tay"), which is played almost exclusively in Ecuador. The players gather on Sunday afternoons. They wear gloves attached to a round, flat wooden paddle with spikes. The players use them to hit a rubber ball back and forth to each other.

The second most popular game is basketball, and Ecuadorians also enjoy playing volleyball. Tennis is becoming increasingly popular, partly due to the success of Ecuadorian tennis player Andrés Gómez, who won the U.S. Open in Men's Doubles in 1986 and the French Open in 1990.

FESTIVALS

ECUADOR'S LONG HISTORY OF CATHOLICISM has combined with its rich indigenous culture to create many festivals. For most Ecuadorians, festival days form the calendar of their vacations, whether because of convenience or because of the simple fact that the *fiestas* ("fee-AIS-tahs") provide the only break from the monotonous struggle to survive.

With the preponderance of religious, national, and local holidays, each month contains one or more festivals somewhere in the country. Ecuadorians observe all of them with great enthusiasm. Some are distinguished by special foods, drinks, and costumes, but generally, fiestas consist of parades or religious processions with lots of people, music, food, and alcohol.

Opposite: **Festival dancing in the Paseo del Chagra.**

Below: **All Souls' Day.**

CALENDAR OF MAJOR HOLIDAYS AND FESTIVALS

January 1	New Year's Day	August 10	Independence Day
January 6	Epiphany	September 1-15	Fiesta del Yamor (Otavalo)
March or April	Carnival	October 9	Guayaquil's Independence Day
March or April	Easter	October 12	Columbus Day or Americas Day
May 1	Labor Day	November 1	All Saints' Day
May 24	Battle of Pichincha	November 2	Day of the Dead
June	Corpus Cristi	November 3	Cuenca's Independence'
June 24	Saint John the Baptist	December 6	Founding of Quito
June 29	Saints Peter and Paul	December 24	Christmas Eve
July 24	Simón Bolívar's Birthday	December 25	Christmas Day
July 25	Founding of Guayaquil	December 28-31	End-of-Year Celebrations

Within a procession of banners and dancers for the Fiesta de San Pedro, some men and women carry roosters in wooden cages or tied to a pole as part of a traditional ceremony called entrega de gallos *("ayn-TRAY-gah day GUY-yohs"), or "delivering roosters." This derives from colonial days, when the dancers would show their loyalty to the landowner by presenting him with the gift of a rooster every year.*

PATRON SAINTS' DAYS

Ecuador observes many religious holidays, both nationally and locally. Each town has a patron saint, in whose honor a special day is celebrated each year. Some of the local patron saint's days have become famous throughout Ecuador for their colorful festivities, which usually begin the night before the actual day of observance. Although the holidays were originally introduced by the Church, they are not somber affairs. Rather the patron saints' days are often characterized by great license.

In the Otavalo area, the festival for *San Juan Bautista*, or Saint John the Baptist, most likely replaced the indigenous celebration of the solstice on June 21. Today the Catholic fiesta lasts nearly a week and is filled with costumes, dancing, and music. The fiesta music often repeats a single refrain over and over again, with slight variations.

El Día de San Juan Bautista is a fiesta for the men, and the men dress up in an astounding variety of costumes, including satirized *gringo* characters with blonde wigs, Mexicans with wide sombreros, and women. Each night, groups of musicians and dancers move from house to house stamping in a circle and reversing direction suddenly. A custom that seems connected to *pacha mama* rituals in Bolivia and Peru consists of throwing rocks at the chapel of San Juan.

Another festival in Imbabura Province and especially in Cotacachi is the fiesta of Saints Peter and Paul, or *San Pedro y Paulo*. While San Juan is the patron saint for the Otavaleños, San Pedro is the patron saint for the other group of indígenas in Imbabura Province. On June 29, hundreds of these people descend on the town of Cayambe, where the patron saint is also San Pedro. The festivals of the three saints sometimes run together for a week or more of celebration.

Opposite: **The San Juan Bautista Festival in Cotacachi.**

An Easter Sunday procession in Cotacachi.

HOLY WEEK AND EASTER

As one of the most important holidays on the Church calendar, Easter (*El Pascua*) presents an occasion for great celebration. It is preceded by Holy Week, or *Semana Santa*. In many towns, costumed worshippers observe Good Friday, two days before Easter, by reenacting the procession of Christ carrying the cross. Religious processions also take place on Holy Saturday and on Easter Sunday.

On Easter Sunday, after mass, the family gathers for a feast consisting of a traditional Ecuadorian soup called *fanseca* ("fahn-SAY-kah"). Fanseca combines ingredients from the lowlands and from the highlands, including onions, peanuts, fish, rice, squash, broad beans, lupine, corn, lentils, beans, peas, and *melloco* ("may-YOH-koh," a highland tuber).

DAY OF THE DEAD

Although the significance of *El Día de Difuntos* ("dee-FOON-tohs") is rather somber, the observance is usually festive in tone. On November 2, the day after All Saints' Day, people all over Ecuador bake small figures of humans and animals made from *masapan*, or bread dough. They take the figures to the cemeteries and place them on the graves of family members, along with paper wreaths and offerings of food and drink.

CORPUS CRISTI

This holiday is usually observed on the Thursday after Trinity Sunday, in honor of the Eucharist. Although celebrated in many parts of Ecuador, it is considered a major fiesta among certain indígenas in the central Sierra. In some communities, traditional dancers with ornate headdresses and embroidered costumes celebrate with music and dance. In Salasaca, the indígenas wear plaster masks, and ribbons and feathers on their hats, and dance along the streets to the next town.

CHRISTMAS

Christmas is a serious religious holiday in Ecuador. One traditional custom is the *Pase del Niño* ("PAH-say del NEEN-yoh"), or the presentation of the Christ child. Especially in the smaller towns and villages, people carry statues of the baby Jesus to the local church, walking in a procession accompanied by musicians and costumed children who represent the nativity. The priest blesses the statues in a special mass, after which the families take them back to their household creches. Christmas trees have become more popular in recent years; but Ecuadorians lavish much more attention on their nativity scenes, which can be quite elaborate.

Many Ecuadorians start celebrating Christmas at the beginning of December. Families hold *novenas* ("noh-BAY-nahs") in the days preceding Christmas. They gather at a different family member's house each evening for prayers and singing. The family concludes the evening's devotions with a party with lots of food and alcohol.

On Christmas Eve, everyone attends the midnight mass, after which they return home to eat and drink the night away. The traditional Christmas drink is *canelazo* ("cah-nay-LAH-soh"), made from hot water, sugarcane alcohol, lemon, and cinnamon. People exchange gifts on Christmas day, and the extended family again assembles for another feast.

The Christmas season finally comes to a conclusion on January 6, with the Festival of the Three Kings, also known as Epiphany. This holiday is primarily for children.

On January 6, children attend a special mass, sing Christmas carols, and march in processions. They may also receive small gifts and watch fireworks.

A dance group at a festival to mark the changing of the mayor.

THE INDIGENOUS FIESTA SYSTEM

For centuries the indígenas of the Sierra have participated in a formalized fiesta system where one person—the wealthiest in the community—is chosen each year to host the patron saint's celebration. Young men assume a particular menial task known as a *cargo* ("KAR-goh"), or "burden." For instance, they might have to clean the church or serve as the night watchman. By the time they are adults, their *cargo* has increased to the level of being responsible for organizing and carrying out the costly festival for the village's patron saint. As a man fulfills his religious obligations, he gains prestige and disposes of his wealth. The host of the fiesta also serves on the town council for the year.

It was once believed that the fiesta system served to insure that no one individual became significantly richer than everyone else. Recently, however, anthropologists have noted that the profits of these celebrations actually went to the Church, who selected the unwilling host of the fiesta.

Since the 1964 land reform, the fiesta system has become less common. Today the festival costs are often paid for through collections and contributions from the community members.

NEW YEAR'S

On the last night of the year, December 31, Ecuadorians say good-bye to *El Año Viejo* and greet *El Año Nuevo*. They light bonfires and stuff old clothes to make life-sized puppets. The puppets are called *los viejos* ("vee-AY-hos") and symbolize the old year; sometimes they are fashioned humorously to represent political figures. Especially in Guayaquil and Esmeraldas, the people display *los viejos* on the main streets of the city and burn them in the bonfires at midnight.

On New Year's Day, *El Año Nuevo*, people go out to dance, masquerade in costumes, and eat and drink.

FOUNDING DAYS

People in Guayaquil, Quito, and Cuenca all go wild celebrating the founding of their cities. They have parades, fireworks, art shows, beauty pageants, and in the Sierra, bullfights. As always, there is plenty of music and dancing in the streets, combined with lots of eating and drinking.

These festivals are quite remarkable for the intensity with which the citizens participate in the events. Open-air concerts are attended by thousands of people, who pack themselves onto the streets so tightly that they can hardly move.

Guayaquil combines the celebration for the Founding of Guayaquil (July 25) with that for Simón Bolívar's birthday (July 24), and celebrations sometimes begin even a few days earlier. The Founding of Cuenca (November 3) is celebrated in conjunction with All Saints' Day and Day of the Dead (November 1–2), which makes this a particularly spectacular festival for the city.

FOOD

ECUADORIAN CUISINE is relatively mild, enlivened by touches of *ají* ("ah-HEE"), a chili sauce that Ecuadorians put on the table at almost every meal. Meals almost always include a starchy food, such as plantains, potatoes, or rice. Plantains, or *plátanos* ("PLAH-tah-nohs"), are the more common cousin of the sweet banana; in taste and texture, however, a plantain is somewhere between potatoes and squash. Plantains are not eaten raw; rather they are boiled, deep-fried, or baked.

Opposite: **Llapingachos** **("ya-peen-GAH-chos")** **are small cheese and po-** **tato cakes served on** **white rice with a fried egg** **and slices of avocado.**

Above: **Meals usually in-** **clude potatoes.**

One of the most influential aspects of the Spanish conquest of the Americas was the wide variety of foods they took back to Europe. The potato, for instance, probably had more of an impact on the world's diet than any other food; it completely changed the basic diet of many European societies.

BANANAS

As the world's largest exporter of bananas, Ecuador enjoys a wide variety of bananas and plantains. Several types of bananas and plantains are grown in the Costa and in the Oriente, including tiny finger bananas (oritas, "oh-REE-tahs"); the yellow eating bananas; the short, fat red eating bananas (*magueños,* "mah-GAY-nyohs"); and large, green cooking plantains (*plátanos*). The plantains are used in different ways, depending on their degree of maturity; they are referred to either as *verde* ("BAYR-day," green and unripe) or *maduro* ("mah-DOO-roh," ripe with a blackened yellow skin). People all over the country eat the starchy fruit in a variety of ways; but they are most popular when deep fried. *Chifles* ("CHEE-flais") are a favorite snack, made from deep-fried green plantains that have been peeled and thinly sliced into chips. Ecuadorians eat them with the same gusto that North Americans apply to potato chips.

FAVORITE DISHES

Ecuadorians favor a lot of fried foods, and they eat rice or potatoes with almost every meal, sometimes together. White rice is usually served plain and sticky but is sometimes prepared as a combination dish with chicken or beef. Ecuadorian cuisine is also characterized by the pervasive use of cilantro, an herb similar to parsley.

Some traditional dishes include *humitas* ("oo-MEE-tahs"), which are sweet corn tamales; *empanadas* ("aim-pan-AH-das"), which are meat-filled pastries; and *choclos* ("CHOH-clohs"), ears of corn toasted in fat. Popular meat dishes include *lechón* ("lay-CHOHN"), or suckling pig, and *cuy* ("KWEE"), or guinea pig. Cuy is a delicacy that dates back to the Inca civilization. Farmers throughout the countryside raise them and roast them whole.

Suckling pigs are roasted whole and are a common sight at marketplaces and on city sidewalks.

MEALTIMES

Ecuadorian families eat most of their meals together, except on occasions when one or more of the family members are unable to return home from work or school for the midday meal. It is not uncommon for the father of the household to skip the midday meal at home, however. Most middle- and upper class families have a maid who either lives in the house or comes to work daily. She prepares all the meals, often with instructions for the menu from the mother of the household.

Ecuadorians eat a light breakfast, especially in the highlands, where the atmosphere is so

A family sits down to lunch together.

thin that they don't like to start the day with a "heavy stomach." Breakfast, *el desayuno* ("day-sai-OON-oh"), usually consists of little more than a white bread roll with white cheese, juice, and coffee; they may occasionally add an egg. Family members often just eat a quick meal by themselves.

The midday meal, *el almuerzo* ("ahl-moo-AIR-soh"), is the largest meal of the day and includes at least three courses. The meal begins with a *sopa* (or in the Costa, with *ceviche*), followed by the main dish, which is accompanied by plenty of rice or potatoes. This may be a *seco* such as a thick lentil stew, or fish or chicken. The *almuerzo* sometimes includes a light salad or a side dish of boiled broad beans or other vegetables. The meal concludes with the *postre* ("POHS-tray"), or dessert, which usually is a serving of fruit, *flan* (a caramel custard), or sweetened, fried plantains.

The family usually sits down to the evening meal, *cena* ("SAY-nah") together. Because Ecuadorians usually work into the evening, the *cena* tends to be light and may consist of no more than grilled cheese sandwiches or flour or corn pancakes. Or they may have a simpler version of the midday meal, eating meat and rice or potatoes, followed by a light *postre*.

REGIONAL COOKING

As in other things, there are many regional variations in Ecuadorian food.

SIERRA Serranos in Ecuador eat a lot of soups and stews made with barley, corn, potatoes, beans, peas, broad beans, squash, quinoa (a highland grain), and *melloco* (a tuber). Corn in Ecuador is usually served on the cob. The cook may also boil the kernels, parch them, or pop them. Popcorn has been popular for centuries in Ecuador.

Soups are generally known as *caldos* or *sopas*, while the thicker stews are known as *secas* ("say-kahs"), meaning "dry." People in the Sierra eat soup every day, and the variations are endless. *Locro* ("LOH-croh"), a "wet" soup, is a traditional Ecuadorian soup made from cheese and potatoes. A fancier version, very popular in the countryside, is made with the heart, liver, and tripe of a cow, sheep, or pig. *Sancocho* ("sahn-COH-choh") is another traditional Ecuadorian stew made with *plátanos* and *choclos* seasoned with cilantro.

An Otavalo cook.

Many highland campesinos, on the other hand, survive on little more than barley, either heavily toasted and made into a flour or lightly toasted and coarsely ground into barley rice. Many eat barley gruel day after day, occasionally flavored with a lump of fat, a bit of sugar or salt, or a piece of onion or potato. When edible weeds are in season, they stew them with the grain. Fava beans are another main meal. In other areas of the Sierra, quinoa serves the same role. Quinoa is native to the Andes and was considered by the Incas to be a sacred grain.

COSTA The Costeño diet consists primarily of coconut milk, peanuts, plantains, noodles, rice, and a lot of seafood and shellfish, including sea bass, shrimp, crab, lobster, and oysters. One of the most popular ways of eating shellfish is in *ceviche*. In *ceviche*, the cook does not actually cook the shellfish; rather, he or she marinates it with onions in lemon or lime juice. Another popular way to prepare fresh fish is to cook it in coconut milk.

Families who depend on wage labor usually eat a poor diet. Rather than rice and beans, as in Central America, poor Costeños subsist on little more than boiled plantains, noodles, and broth. They eat few greens or protein, and eggs and meat are luxuries.

ORIENTE Oriente cuisine is very similar to that of the Costa but includes more game, and river fish such as piranha and catfish instead of seafood. The indígenas of the Oriente subsist primarily on manioc, accompanied by peanuts, fish, game, and even certain grubs, which are either eaten alive and raw or toasted. While such fare as beetle larvae is relatively uncommon in Westernized countries, it is a valuable source of protein.

As in the Costa, *plátanos* are commonly eaten. One popular way of preparing them is to boil and mash them into a drink called *chucula* ("choo-KOO-lah"), similar to a banana milkshake. When entertaining visitors, the Quichua-speaking indígenas also use plantains to make a deliciously spicy stew with catfish or game such as the large rodent known as a *paca*. The Waorani do not hunt large animals such as deer because they believe that these animals are spirits.

Shellfish for sale in the Costa.

DRINKS

Ecuador produces an abundance of fruit, including the naranjilla, *a small, green orange; the* mamey, *an oval fruit with brown, bark-like skin and a rich, orange pulp; and the* cherimoya, *a sugar custard apple with green skin and a white pulp.*

A street vendor preparing a treat made of crushed ice with syrup.

Tap water in Ecuador is not safe, so many people drink carbonated mineral water, sodas, or juice. The variety of fruit juices in Ecuador is mindboggling. People make them fresh for breakfast, drinking a different kind every morning. The most common types of juice are blackberry, orange, grapefruit, pineapple, passion fruit, *guanabana*, melon, watermelon, papaya, and *naranjilla*, which tastes like a bitter orange.

Ecuadorians prepare their coffee by boiling it for hours, until it is reduced to a thick syrup. They store it in a small glass bottle on the table; when they want a cup of coffee, they pour a small amount of the coffee syrup into a cup, and fill it up the rest of the way with hot milk or water.

The most common type of alcoholic drink, *aguardiente* ("ah-gwa-ar-dee-AIN-tay") or "fire-water," is made from sugarcane alcohol. Rum and beer are also very popular. During fiestas and at Christmas time, people make a sort of hot toddy made with *aguardiente* and cinnamon, with a touch of lemon.

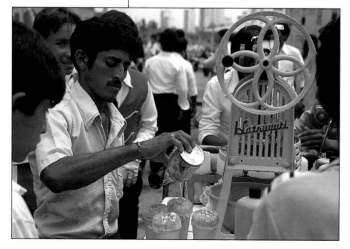

Many indígenas make a traditional, mildly alcoholic drink called *chicha* ("CHEE-cha") by mixing freshly ground corn with boiling water and allowing the mixture to ferment. The indígenas of the Oriente make a thick, slightly alcoholic mash drink as well, which the Waorani call *tepae*. Manioc *tepae* is the staple food for the Waorani. The women break up the cooked tubers with their fingers, put some into their mouth, chew it, and then

spit it back into the pot. It is then allowed to ferment for 48 hours. The resulting flavor and consistency is similar to buttermilk, with a slightly alcoholic zest.

A drink vendor in Guayaquil.

CEVICHE

1 lb. (.45 kg) raw shrimp
1 large red onion
4–5 cups fresh squeezed lime juice
unbuttered, salted popcorn

tabasco sauce to taste
juice of one orange

Clean the shrimp and set aside. Slice the onion very thinly into rings. Salt the onions and barely cover with boiling water. (This cures the onion and takes away the sting without taking away the crispness.)

Toss the shrimp with the onion, and cover the entire combination with freshly squeezed lime juice. Add a few drops of tabasco sauce and the orange juice. Cover the bowl and let the mixture sit overnight in the refrigerator, until thoroughly marinated. This "cooks" the shrimp, turning it pink with the acid of the lime juice. No heating is necessary.

Serve, accompanied by a side dish of unbuttered, salted popcorn. As you eat, toss some of the popcorn into the juice to sop it up.

KITCHENS

In middle- and upper-class homes, the maid presides over the kitchen but in conjunction with the mother of the household. The modern kitchen contains a refrigerator and a gas or electric range and oven. In many homes with refrigerators, however, even educated Ecuadorians do not bother to refrigerate such foods as cheese, meat, and milk. Automatic dishwashers are not very common because so many families employ a domestic worker to do the dishes. (The same is true for automatic clothes washers.)

In urban areas, moreover, the municipal supply of running water is often unreliable or scarce, even in homes equipped with water pipes. Thus, Ecuadorians conserve their water carefully when washing the dishes or clothes. They also tend to use cold water for these purposes.

Many lower-class homes in the cities and in the countryside simply lack electricity and running water. Indigenous people usually cook over open fires, while sitting or crouching on the ground. Missionaries have tried to introduce the raised platform ovens that many campesinos use, but with little success.

MARKETPLACES

Ecuador's marketplaces reflect the diversity of income, social status, and ethnicity within the society. There are essentially four types of marketplaces. There is the indoor, modernized supermarket and the traditional outdoor market with its rows of stalls or blankets of food. The outdoor markets are usually held weekly with the animal market and the crafts market.

At one end of the open-air marketplace is the meat market, with tables and booths of freshly slaughtered beef, lamb, chicken, pork, turkey, *cuy*, goat, and prepared sausages of all kinds. Next to the meat market is the produce market, filled with row upon row of colorfully stocked booths, tables, and blankets upon the ground, all offering an astounding variety of grains, fruits, and vegetables.

In addition, these marketplaces also offer bread, cheese, baskets, plasticware, flowers, rope, thread, bandages, aspirin and antacids, knives, sunglasses, scissors, toothpaste, and other mundane items.

Located near the food markets is the crafts market, which sells whatever crafts are locally renowned, in addition to products from elsewhere in Ecuador. A bit farther away is usually located the livestock market.

Bargaining is a fundamental part of the traditional marketplace. In choosing which vendors to buy from, the shopper judges the quality and price of individual offerings. Upon finding a suitable selection of plátanos, for instance, she will then ask the vendor how much they cost. After the vendor quotes a figure (usually inflated), the shopper responds by offering a lower price. They bargain over the goods with shrewd efficiency.

A vegetable market in Coca.

Opposite: **A rural kitchen combining cooking space with guinea pig quarters.**

121

ECUADOR

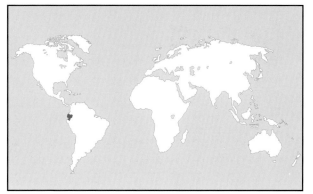

QUICK NOTES

OFFICAL NAME
Republic of Equador

LAND AREA
105,037 square miles (272,045 sq km)

POPULATION
10,741,000 (1992 estimate)

POPULATION DENSITY
104 per square mile (39.5 per sq km)

CAPITAL
Quito

MAJOR CITIES
Guayaquil (1,500,000)
Quito (1,100,000)

PROVINCES
Azuay, Bolívar, Cañar, Carchi, Cotopaxi, Chimborazo, El Oro, Esmeraldas, Guayas, Imbabura, Loja, Los Ríos, Manabí, Morona Santiago, Napo, Pastaza, Pichincha, Sucumbíos, Tungurahua, Zamora Chinchipe, Archipiélago de Colón (Galápagos)

MAJOR RIVERS
Río Guayas, Río Pastaza, Río Napo

MAJOR LAKE
Lago San Pablo

FLAG
Three horizontal stripes of yellow, blue, and red

NATIONAL SYMBOL
The coat of arms, which displays a condor, Mount Chimborazo, and a steamer boat

NATIONAL BIRD
Andean Condor

HIGHEST POINT
Mt. Chimborazo (20,556 feet, 6,265 m)

LANGUAGES
Spanish (official)
Quichua (major)
Shuar/Ashuar (major)
Waorani
Cofán
Siona-Secoya
Zaporoan

MAJOR RELIGION
Roman Catholicism

CURRENCY
Sucre ($1 = 1,875 sucre)

MAIN EXPORTS
Petroleum, bananas, coffee

IMPORTANT ANNIVERSARIES
Founding of Guayaquil, July 25
Independence Day, August 10
Columbus Day/Americas Day , October 12
Founding of Quito, December 6

CURRENT PRESIDENT
Sixto Durán Ballén

GLOSSARY

campesino ("kam-pay-SEE-noh")
Peasant or farmer.

caudillo ("cow-DEE-oh")
The person who guides and commands people as a leader.

compadres ("kom-PAHD-rays")
Godparents.

cordillera ("kor-dee-YAY-rah")
Mountain chain.

Costa
The coastal region.

Costeño
An inhabitant of the Costa, or coastal region.

galápago ("gal-AH-pah-goh")
Tortoise.

Gross National Product (GNP)
The Gross National Product is the total market value of the goods and services produced by a nation's economy, including receipts from overseas. The Gross Domestic Product (GDP) does not include receipts from overseas.

hacienda ("ah-see-EHN-dah")
Large estate, usually in the Sierra.

hacendado ("ah-sen-DAH-do")
Hacienda owner.

indígena ("een-DEE-hay-nah")
Indigenous person.

la gente buena ("la HEN-tay BWAY-nah")
The "good" or "respectable" people, referring to the middle and upper classes.

mestizo ("mais-TEE-soh")
A person of mixed white and indigenous ancestry.

montuvio ("mohn-TOO-vyo")
A person of mixed black, Hispanic, and indigenous ancestry.

mulatto
A person of mixed black and white ancestry.

El Niño
A climatological phenomenon that occurs every 6–7 years and causes storms, flooding, and landslides.

Oriente
The eastern, or Amazon, region.

páramo ("PAHR-ah-moh")
Highland area above 11,500 feet (3,500 m).

Quichua ("KEE-chwa")
An Ecuadorian dialect of Quechua, an indigenous language spoken in Andean South America.

Serrano
An inhabitant of the Sierra.

Sierra
The central, mountain region.

zambo ("TSAHM-boh")
A person of mixed black and indigenous ancestry.

BIBLIOGRAPHY

Corkill, David. *Ecuador.* Sant Barbara, California: ABC Clio, 1989.

Hanratty, Dennis Michael. *Ecuador: A Country Study.* Washington: U.S. Government Printing Office, 1991.

Lerner Publications. *Ecuador—In Pictures.* Minneapolis, Minnesota: Lerner Publications, 1987.

Odijk, Pamela. *The Incas.* Englewood Cliffs, New Jersey: Silver Burdett, 1990.

Thomsen, Moritz. *The Saddest Pleasure: A Journey on Two Rivers.* St. Paul, Minnesota: Graywolf Press, 1990.

INDEX

INDEX

INDEX

Picture Credits